WOUNDS *in the heart*

Wounds in the heart

The Healing Power of Forgiveness

Dr. Javier Schlatter

www.scepterpublishers.org

Cover and text design by Rose Design

ISBN: 978-1-59417-225-0

Printed in the United States of America

Contents

CHAPTER 1

What Is Forgiveness?

"Forgiveness is not a perfect thing, if it is not converted into generous love."

—B. L. de Argensola, *Sonnets*, XCIV

". . . has shaken and awakened the most noble capacities of the human heart, in particular the capacity to forgive and to respond with magnanimity to an injury suffered."

—Fyodor Dostoyevsky, *The Insulted and Humiliated*

Many people consider medicine a vocation of service, of helping others. I am not going to contradict this, especially since it is one of the principal motives that led me to dedicate myself to psychiatry. But as the years go by, I see more and more clearly that I am the one who has benefited from that decision. One of the reasons reinforcing this conviction is precisely the reason for this book.

One ordinary day about a year ago, as I finished the last consultation of the evening, I began to think about what I had just witnessed.[1] Nestor, age twenty-four, the youngest of six brothers, had told me several sessions before that when he was a small child one of his brothers had abused him for several years. He had never spoken about this to anyone, and although he had gotten used to "living" with his memories, he suspected he could not be happy until he had forgiven his brother. He had never felt able to do that, and the day his brother left home was a real relief for him. Later, though, his brother returned home. Nestor understood that the time had come for him to make the attempt, and he asked my help. But I had doubts. Was Nestor prepared for this? Wouldn't it be even more damaging if he tried and failed? Weren't there other ways of solving the problem?

Also fresh in my mind was a conversation with Soledad and Sergio a few days earlier. They were a well-matched married couple, or at least so it seemed. Soledad had just found out accidentally that, years earlier, Sergio had a passing affair on a business trip. He admitted it while giving his word that he'd never been unfaithful at any other time. They came for help because Soledad was suffering immense pain and had totally rejected her spouse.

---

1. The narratives in this book about patients I have seen in my office are based on real cases, sometimes combining two or more stories, although the names and identifying details have been changed to safeguard the privacy of those involved.

Sergio suggested marriage therapy, and Soledad agreed in hopes of saving the marriage. After a few sessions, she faltered. She felt incapable of forgiving him. She abandoned the therapy and began a process of separation. I was frustrated because I believed they could reconcile and continue to be happy. But was his affair really something unforgivable? And if she forgave him, would it show a lack of self-respect on her part? Was her difficulty in transcending this betrayal due to the betrayal or due to her? Is mutual love a sufficient grounding for forgiveness? Can some injuries only be forgiven by a person of faith?

Studying forgiveness, I have been surprised by its great depth and richness. World literature abounds with stories of people who lacked the will or ability to forgive, but there are fewer accounts of persons celebrated for being good at forgiving. Still, we do have the story of Jean Valjean in *Les Miserables*, Victor Hugo's 1862 masterpiece. Here is a young man with a big heart, orphaned at an early age. A disproportionately long sentence for stealing bread to feed his hungry nieces and nephew and the experience of prison fill his heart with hatred and misery. Once free, he suffers society's rejection as an ex-convict. In his desperation, he encounters the understanding and later the forgiveness of a bishop. His heart is changed, and from then on it is he who helps and has pity on other people, even at the risk of his own freedom and his very life. At length he not only ends his life at peace with himself but makes it possible for other people to forgive and share in that interior peace. In contrast to Jean Valjean is the police official, Javert, who relentlessly pursues Valjean, ignoring his signs of goodness and repentance, even when Valjean saves him from being killed by revolutionaries. Blinded by his rigid sense of duty and justice, Javert despairs at the evidence of his error and his miserable meanness.

In the pages that follow, we shall examine the principal characteristics of this tremendously human and overwhelming reality called forgiveness and review how it has been understood and lived by the major cultures and religions.

AN INTRODUCTION TO THE CONCEPT OF FORGIVENESS

There is an old saying that to err is human. If man lived alone, he would correct his own errors, suffering the consequences in his own flesh and rectifying his mistakes, or not. But fortunately man is a social animal. That means one's mistakes can harm or provoke suffering in others.[2]

---

2. Robert Spaemann speaks in his book *Happiness and Benevolence* (New York: Bloomsbury T&T Clark, 2005) of what he calls "ontological forgiveness," motivated by recognizing in the other person one's own finiteness, the source of his injustice in dealing with oneself. The conclusion is that we all stand in need of being forgiven.

At other times, it is as Ovid said: "I see and I desire the better: I follow the worse."[3] Not only do we cause injury to others, we place of our interest above theirs, or even directly seek to do them evil.

We have all suffered offenses or injuries, whether physical or moral. On such occasions we often think spontaneously of returning the insult or injury. That reaction can be regarded as natural, though not necessarily automatic. As Victor Frankl points out, there is a space for freedom between the stimulus and the response, and in that space is our growth and happiness.[4] Forgiveness is the root. The spontaneous reaction of returning evil for evil is translated into a negative moral or physical response of anger mixed with sorrow, which repels the attack. We want the aggressor to stop, and we try to protect ourselves from another act of aggression. Sometimes we do not respond actively, but whether we do or don't—and especially the latter—the pain caused by the offense usually turns into anger and hatred against the aggressor.[5]

---

3. Ovid, *Metamorphoses*, VII, 21.

4. Viktor Frankl, *Man's Search for Meaning* (Boston: Beacon Press, 2014).

5. Anger is one of the strongest passions. It leads us to pursue what is difficult or costly, perceived as a mixture of good and evil, and has two objectives: to remedy the evil and require satisfaction, and to seek vengeance or reparation as a desired good. According to St. Thomas, it is the most "human" of the passions, since it is very much allied with reason inasmuch as it requires comparing weighing the damage and

If that pain lasts for a long time, it is transformed into resentment. Hatred tends to last just as love does unless we do something to mitigate it or stop nourishing it. Any new stimulus related to an injury received typically recalls it to our minds and makes us return, intellectually and emotionally, to the "scene of the crime." In this way, unless we intervene to prevent it, a kind of a loop is established that can go on repeating and perpetuating itself indefinitely. In those circumstances it is as if time stands still and we remain trapped in the loop, anchored to this painful point. While we might then suppose that the offense or aggression is causing our unhappiness, more often it is our own resentment that produces this result.

From this perspective, forgiveness and trust[6] are the two powers human beings need most in order to live in society. Man needs forgiveness and trust in his quality as a relational being, "a being for others," living with them in a stable manner.

---

measuring the satisfaction demanded—all things that require use of the intellect. On the other hand, although the passions are said to be blind, anger is undoubtedly the most likely to result in an outburst in which one's conscience is clouded. See Walter Farrell, O.P., *A Companion to the Summa,* Vol. II. First Part, I, II. QQ. 1–67 (Haines City, Fla.: Revelation Insight, first edition 2010).

6. On this matter Hannah Arendt has an excellent analysis in *The Human Condition* (Chicago: University of Chicago Press, 1998).

We need trust from the time we are born.[7] Due to our limitations, we lose our insecurity and acquire trust with experience, with growth in knowledge, etc. But there is always tomorrow, something yet to come, something new to explore or experience. We must therefore trust in what we have learned and in some way take for granted.

I have to trust that others will act as they have up to now: that the bus will arrive at the scheduled time; that when I go to bed tonight I will fall asleep, etc. These are acts of faith and trust, more or less explicit, which allow me to live with the confidence that everything is going to be "normal" as foreseen. Confidence is necessary to be able to move on in life—without having to make certain that, as it were, the nails are still well anchored in the wall.

Something similar happens with forgiveness. We need it for daily living. Offenses have the attractive power of evil, and injuries incline us to self-preservation and self-pity, both of which lead us to focus on the act of aggression. Someone meant by

---

7. According to Erik Erikson's evolutionary psychiatry account, we acquire trust during the first twelve to eighteen months of life. This may be greater or lesser, depending on the care we receive, the satisfaction of our nutritional needs, being carried, nurtured, and reassured. From this comes the later disposition to trust others, a basic trust in ourself, and the capacity to receive from and depend on others and instill trust.

nature to live in the present while looking forward to the future requires forgiveness to avoid getting bogged down in the pitfalls of living. Otherwise one would spend life with a conditioned freedom, attached to a chain linking one, by means of suffering, to past offenses or guilt. Thanks to forgiveness, we can liberate ourselves from that chain and can continue moving ahead.

If I remained attached to the loop of ill-feeling, I would not only feel the same pain over and over again but would acquire a perception of eternity marked by impotence and despair. I would feel hatred toward the aggressor, a suffering involving the pain and failure to break free from negative emotions that might be tempered if expressed in an adequate form. Hatred, like envy, has great difficulty in this regard. Complaining or weeping can reduce pain, but what gets rid of the hatred?

The normal thing is first to associate the aggression with the aggressor: Who did it? Hatred then demands vengeance, which, far from eliminating the pain, gives rise to more. At this point, the suffering person finds himself in a situation similar to those condemned to the last circle of the Inferno in Dante's hell.[8] He wants to cry, to vent his anguish

---

8. "We followed to where the ice cruelly oppressed other condemned ones. . . . Mourning it did not allow them to weep, and the suffering that they found in the obstacle over their eyes turned within them to

and grief, but he realizes with horror that he cannot shed tears. Undoubtedly, these would relieve his pain, but as soon as they appear, they produce a piercing pain that increases his suffering and, with time, his despair.[9] Nor would it help to deny the negative emotions and feelings. This happens, for example, when the victim adopts a defense mechanism leading to identification with the aggressor or even, through immaturity, to the conclusion that perhaps it's he himself who is to blame.

Upon finding oneself in this situation, what outlet is there for one who has been hurt? Revenge? I see that this hurts me, and the aggressor remains. It is necessary to "dissolve" this aggression–aggressor association in order to forgive the aggressor. It seems reasonable that the injured person take measures to avoid being harmed again, even if only through his natural instinct for survival. But is this the same as responding to aggression with hatred?

---

increase their pain, for the first tears formed a barrier, and like a blinder covered the whole eye underneath the eyelids" (canto 33, vv. 91–99). Further on, one of the condemned directs a request to the two travelers: "O cruel souls who are visiting the lowest depths! Take from my eyes this hard veil so that I can relieve myself of the sorrow that fills my heart before the tears freeze over again" (Dante Alighieri, *The Divine Comedy*, "The Inferno," vv. 110–114).

9. "Part of every misery is, so to speak, the misery's shadow or reflection: the fact that you don't merely suffer but have to keep on thinking about the fact that you suffer." C.S. Lewis, *A Grief Observed* (San Francisco: HarperOne, 2009).

We know how spirals of violence develop. It's very easy for a victim to quickly turn into an aggressor and the roles reverse. Through pain and hatred we pass from not forgiving to vengeance. The suffering-hatred linkage in the victim's mind now goes on to tie the victim to the aggressor in an unending dynamic process: offense, pain, hatred, vengeance, and a new offense.

But if not revenge, what other solution is available? Only one, surely the most enriching and positive: forgiveness. Forgiveness is the hatchet that severs the pain-vengeance cycle, freeing both victim and aggressor. In Victor Hugo's story, Jean Valjean is freed by the Bishop Myriel's forgiveness and eventually is able to obtain this same benefit for others—except Javert, who, full of despair, can't believe in that possibility and decides to end his life.

Some authors distinguish two types of forgiveness. One is genuine forgiveness in which the individual who has been wronged desires to forgive. This might be called forgiveness for both parties. The other is forgiveness primarily for the benefit of the one who pardons by becoming free from the damage-pain cycle. Thus released from that emotional burden, one can move on. There is nothing wrong with it, but it lacks the fullness of the first kind.

In both cases, the person is able to turn the page and get on with his or her life. This is not the same as acting as if nothing has happened. It is more like turning a page of a story in which the new episode is related to what came before it. Forgiving does not guarantee that everything will now be as it was. The past inevitably has shaped the present, just as the present will shape the future. Moreover, in forgiving an aggressor, one distinguishes between him and his offense and restores dignity to him: *You are a person who has injured me, but above all you are a person. I forgive so that you will not do this again (love), and I forgive you as an offender like myself (compassion).*

Forgiveness then produces a real change. In the same way that promises are not described but instead are made, forgiveness is more than a declaration: it supposes an action—that of breaking the loop and establishing a new relationship. In the same way, as we will see later, asking for forgiveness can do more than erase guilty feelings—it can remove the objective moral reality of guilt.[10]

In summary, although forgiveness is basically a personal reality, it is necessary for the sake of conserving and enriching interpersonal relationships in order to sustain the social beings we are. Its essentially positive content does not consist simply in repairing something broken but in enriching both

---

10. In this sense, forgiveness, like a promise, is a performative act that changes the state of things in the world, as opposed to a declarative act that only describes them.

the one who forgives and the one forgiven. A life without forgiveness, a life without love, is inhuman and even hateful.

CHARACTERISTICS OF FORGIVENESS

During the Fiftieth International Eucharistic Congress in Dublin in the summer of 2012, a letter was read from Sister Genevieve, a survivor of the Rwanda genocide of 1994. The religious sister spoke of the pain and hatred in her soul; her family had been hauled into a church along with others and murdered there. Later an unexpected event changed her life. She was visiting a prison when one of the prisoners who had participated in the slayings and knew she had lost her family approached her and asked for forgiveness on his knees. "A feeling of pity and compassion invaded me," she recalled. She lifted him up, embraced him, weeping, and told him: "You are my brother and always will be." Then she felt that a great burden had been taken from her and replaced by interior peace. "I thanked the man I was embracing. To my great surprise, he shouted: 'Justice should do its work and condemn me to death, but now I am free!'"

In this case the manifestation of repentance set into motion the forgiveness of an injured person. But not everyone will forgive in such situations, nor can all of the possible responses be considered authentic forgiveness. Let us consider the fundamental characteristics of genuine forgiveness.

Forgiveness is free. Forgiveness that is forced is not true forgiveness. I can put up with a debt, be indulgent, act as if nothing had happened, but this doesn't mean I have forgiven. Freedom is an essential condition—both "freedom to" choose to forgive and "freedom of" the person who grants forgiveness.

Forgiveness involves taking a position in regard to an injury received that brings one to want to transcend it and resolve the negative emotions accompanying it. The injured party makes a choice regarding the one who inflicted the injury, and the choice is the seed of something new, a new relationship.

On the other hand, injuries that go untreated reduce one's freedom. They can make one either insensitive or inaccessible to others or hypersensitive and susceptible. As Alex Pattakos, a disciple of Victor Frankl, once said, "Forgiveness is the key that opens the mental prison cell and liberates you, gives you control. Because the more anger or rage you have towards others, the more power they have over you."[11]

11. Alex Pattakos, interview in the newspaper *La Vanguardia*, February 24, 2008.

Pattakos recalled what Nelson Mandela said of his release from prison after nearly three decades: "On coming out and seeing all those people, I felt great anger for the 27 years of life that they had robbed me of; but then the spirit of Jesus said to me: 'Nelson, when you were in prison you were free. Now that you are free, do not turn yourself into a prisoner of yourself.'" Forgiveness, then, is free and freeing.

Being free is not something effortless. Excessive readiness to forgive can raise the suspicion of which a poet speaks. "For in part it may seem that one consents, if one forgives lightly and easily."[12]

Forgiveness is freely extended in the face of an objective evil caused intentionally. One who forgives must recognize that the offense is objectively evil and directed toward oneself. One does not "forgive" a policeman who tickets one for illegal parking, or a nurse who gives a painful injection that cures one. The hurt must be objectively bad, with a negative value.

In Nestor's case, to forgive the brother who had abused him in childhood, he had to overcome his feelings of guilt. Thinking he was at fault for not having defended himself better, he was prevented

12. Alonso de Ercilla y Zúñiga, *La Araucana. XXXII, estr. 66.*

from seeing clearly the objective evil of the harm he had suffered. This shame for his supposed guilt increased his humiliation and tied him more to the evil he had suffered.

Forgiveness is active. The one who forgives must overcome the resistance caused by the negative emotions arising from the injury. One must make a real effort to renounce vengeance, separating the aggressor from the aggression, valuing the good that is in the aggressor, having compassion on him, constructing a new framework of the relationship that goes beyond the previous one, and then accepting this new relationship. The greater the aggression and the smaller one's capacity for love, the greater must one's decisiveness be.

Except for minor offenses or larger ones between persons who love one another, there must be a clear decision to undertake forgiveness and carry it out to the end. This can start with benevolence toward the person or from the perception that the weight will become even more costly and unbearable if one does not forgive. Although someone may say he lacks the strength to forgive, forgiveness remains the best solution if and when it becomes possible.

Forgiveness is gratuitous. Forgiveness should be granted without looking for anything in exchange, although usually it brings with it an undeniable and gratifying liberation.[13] That it is gratuitous and free does not mean, however, that there are no motives for doing or not doing it. In fact, some authors distinguish between *intentional* and *emotional* forgiveness: in the first, although the mind decides to forgive, the heart holds back, at least initially. *Emotional* forgiveness is the more perfect, for it presupposes a change in one's feelings as well. Probably the most compelling reasons for forgiving are the moral ones—we know it is not morally good to harbor resentment or hate even toward someone who has hurt us. From an affective perspective, this is someone we appreciate and, even though he or she has hurt us, our estimation is stronger than the hurt. From an emotional perspective, we feel bad because of these negative emotions toward the offender, and in order to be and feel well, we must get rid of that weight and forgive, even at the expense of our right to justice or revenge. Gratuitousness is demonstrated, for example, when someone forgives the one who has just hurt him or her, even before the other party can ask forgiveness. Doing that shows a great capacity for love.

13. Some authors hold that forgiveness always serves a purpose (rescue, redemption, reconciliation, salvation) or tries to reestablish a state of normality (psychological, social, national, etc.). Forgiveness obviously takes place in response to a previous reality, but it contains a power to enrich beyond the recovery of what was lost or spoiled.

Ron McClary was sixteen when, fleeing the scene of a robbery in Columbus, Ohio, he shot Tom Hayes, the policeman who was pursuing him, leaving him a paraplegic with multiple health complications. A priest who was Tom's friend asked if he had forgiven the boy who shot him. He answered that he had already done that while lying bleeding in the street. "I thought I would die, and I didn't want to come before Almighty God with hatred in my heart. So I prayed that God would take both of us to heaven." The policeman continued to pray for the rest of his life for the aggressor. Ron spent twenty-four years in prison and, already middle-aged, developed multiple sclerosis. The same priest went to see him and told him Tom had forgiven him and prayed for him every day. Ron admitted he still had nightmares about the event. In time, he decided to be baptized, and on the day of Ron's first holy Communion, the priest asked the policeman's widow if she forgave the man who shot her husband. For thirty-three years she had been unable to do that. But now, hearing his choked-up request for forgiveness, she approached his wheelchair and told him, "I forgive you."

Many motives can be present at the moment of forgiving. Some authors emphasize the victim's desire to overcome negative thoughts, emotions, and behavior—that is, to combat the rage, resentment, constant recalling of the offense, and the desiring and seeking of revenge. Most studies stress the dimension of benevolence—sentiments of empathy, compassion, love, and so on. Other authors, inclining to a middle option, hold that forgiveness has positive elements only in the case of significant relationships.

Forgiveness restores dignity to both the victim and the aggressor. To forgive, it is necessary to go beyond the offense and the offender. Although right now my attention may be focused on the pain or its cause, I must make an effort to recall that a human being is more than his guilt. Yes, what happened to me was unjust, unmerited, objectively evil, and humiliating. But to retain my dignity, I must freely forgive and recognize the dignity of the offender.

Soledad, as we have seen, felt unable to forgive Sergio, despite his apparently sincere repentance and the fact that what happened was an isolated incident. Soledad's worst pain was Sergio's failure to be faithful to an essential commitment, but there was also the humiliation arising from his wish to continue living "as if nothing had happened." Is it better not to forgive some deeds? Are some actually unforgivable? This dilemma frequently arises in cases involving severe violence or sexual abuse. Encouraging the victims to forgive might make them more vulnerable to new abuse. Those who defend this view forget that forgiveness does not rule out doing justice, the punishing of the offender, taking defensive measures, and rendering assistance to the victim to emerge strengthened from the aggression.

Forgiveness can even go beyond justice. The word *pardon* (or forgiveness) comes from the Latin *per-donare.* The prefix *per* gives greater intensity to the word *donare* (to give). As applied to the relationship of offender and victim, to pardon or forgive means to give the other more than is expected—something positive that has not been merited and is given in a gratuitous way.

Some authors concentrate on the victim's renunciation of the right to resentment. Although the one offended knows he has that right, he "makes an effort to consider the offender with benevolence, compassion and even love, recognizing at the same time that this offender has given up his right to them."[14]

This explains why it is so inadequate to define forgiveness as merely remitting a debt. On the contrary, forgiveness means replacing a destructive

14. Etienne Mullet, "Perdón y Terapia (Forgiveness and Therapy)," in *Psicologia Clinica Basada en la Evidencia,* Francisco J. Labrador and Maria Crespo, ed. (Madrid: Piramide, 2012), pp. 137–152.

behavior with a constructive one: re-creating the relationship between aggressor and victim and purifying one's memory of rancor and revenge.

CULTURAL ASPECTS

The study of forgiveness is relatively new. Those who write about it usually mention a first stage that ended in the 1980s. Authors like Piaget then paid particular attention to forgiveness's moral aspects. Since then, others like Fitzgibbons have explored its psychosocial foundations and carried out more rigorous research, at both the individual and group levels. More recently, writers have focused on forgiveness as a help in overcoming negative situations, or on its efficacy in repairing wounds inflicted in interpersonal or group relationships; they have therefore viewed it from a more relational or social perspective.

One way of approaching the cultural aspects of this reality is to consider what happens in environments that don't view forgiveness as a remedy that fully repairs harm. Clearly, in any culture, people who are close to one another, who love or simply respect one another, can forgive little everyday things. But what happens when the offenses are of a deeper sort? What consequences does a limited capacity to forgive have for interpersonal relationships?

If such offenses are not forgiven, they usually remain in one's memory, at least in its emotional part. Each person involved will store up a group of offenses that will influence each one's other relationships. These injuries can be "transmitted" between generations, like a kind of virus, accumulating and giving rise to an increasingly disintegrated society. People in such societies bear the emotional weight of negative emotions such as anger, fury, rancor, resentment, humiliation, and impotence.

The network of intertwined injuries creates a climate of suspicion and vulnerability, resulting in people expecting future harm. The response is to live much of the time in the past, filtering present and future expectations through the medium of bad experiences and open wounds.

Living without forgiveness, imprisoned by injuries and offenses, very often leads to vengeance. An injured person may feel a certain satisfaction in seeing an aggressor pay for the harm he has done. In a social context when there is no forgiveness, an injured person will relieve his ire and moderate his grief by passing on his injury. Experience shows that this leads to an unending spiral of aggression and violence. In contrast to the freedom that comes from forgiving, someone engaged in vengeance generally is led by his or her passions, with little or no use of freedom. This is more like animal behavior than the behavior of a rational being.

What role has forgiveness played throughout history in various civilizations? Is it part of all cultures? Is it an anthropological, "super-cultural" element? Are there inter-cultural differences?

In ancient Greek culture, forgiveness did not exist as such, although the Greeks did recognize indulgence, compassion, and sympathy. If, however, someone acted contrary to the gods, for example, he would suffer a corresponding punishment administered in an exemplary manner. Socrates thought his false accusers were doing themselves a greater evil than they were inflicting on him. Instead of desiring vengeance, he therefore had compassion on them, believing it preferable to suffer injustice than to commit it.

Plato did not recognize the existence of guilt, since in his view one who is unjust is so unconsciously, inasmuch as wrong behavior is the result of a mistake. If therefore someone harms me, I should have compassion on him because of his "error." Probably this person's body, the source of evil, has deceived his soul.

Seneca took a position closer to Socrates. He saw taking pity as the basis for forgiveness. "The man who has offended you is either stronger or weaker than you: if he is weaker, spare him; if he is stronger, spare yourself."[15]

Roman law went beyond the Hebrews' Talion law—"an eye for an eye"—and opened the possibility of agreed-upon compensation for the one offended by the one offending; only in the absence of agreement would "an eye for an eye" come into play. Later, agreement became mandatory and the offense a source of obligations, signaling a further distancing from the Talion law.

At present, the idea and practice of forgiveness have not yet reached some cultures, while in other cases forgiveness has been reduced to superficial consolation of a sentimental-spiritual kind that helps one bear an offense. In Western societies, cultural or sociological tendencies may be changing the nature of forgiveness or making it more difficult. These include:

- ***The tendency to autonomy.*** In cases of conflict, people tend to shift their focus to a different person: instead of learning to "get along with you," I will "get along with myself" or seek someone else.

15. Lucius Annasus Seneca, *On Anger*, III, 5.8.

- ***An abundance of superficial relationship networks founded on mutual interest.*** The result can be ignoring a gratuitous act like forgiving, especially when it requires personal effort: "Why should I forgive him after what he has done to me?" Opposed to working things out as friends, a person will seek another relationship and resolve things this way.
- ***Over-reliance on the judicial system—bringing charges against a family member, a teacher, neighbors, etc.***—when the matter could be settled in ways like dialogue or forgiveness, which are essential to real and constructive human relationships.
- ***The tendency to create "camps" and see life in terms of winning or losing.*** Winning is valued over human relationships—and even over truth.

These tendencies have at least three sources. The first is *relativism*, which denies the objective goodness or badness of actions. This subjectivism tends to cloud or even erase guilt and trivialize evil, and where there is no guilt, there is no need for repentance and forgiveness.

The second is *individualism* or radical personal autonomy. If I am autonomous, I don't need anyone's forgiveness, and it's immaterial to me if someone suffers because of some aspect of my behavior. The autonomous person doesn't need others to be happy. This attitude makes it difficult for such a person to put himself in someone else's place and prevents gratuitous forgiving, allowing only a version of forgiveness that expresses power and more nearly resembles clemency.[16]

Finally there is *hedonism* or the direct seeking of what is pleasant, which leads one to avoid suffering. Besides the pain caused by the offense, there is the pain of forgiveness, which is sometimes greater than the pain of the offense.[17] In order to ask forgiveness, one must recognize the truth, repent, manifest the repentance, make reparation if it is required, and commit oneself to not repeating the offense. Fleeing pain, one may seek alternatives to forgiveness—sterile substitutes that perpetuate the wounds.

But despite these negative social tendencies, there also is a growing tendency to seek forgiveness for the sake of reconciliation.

---

16. Some authors emphasize the narcissism typical in the West at the end of the twentieth century, expressed in a tendency to individualism, competitiveness, and an emphasis on personal achievement. This presents an obstacle to forgiveness, which is often seen as a sign of weakness and lack of character. See Paul Vitz, *Psychology as Religion: The Cult of Self-Worship* (Grand Rapids, Mich.: Eerdmans, 1994).

17. "Guilt must be worked through, healed, and thus overcome. Forgiveness exacts a price—first of all from the person who forgives. He must overcome within himself the evil done to him, he must, as it were, burn it interiorly and in so doing renew himself. As a result, he also involves the other, the trespasser, in this process of transformation, of inner purification, and both parties, suffering all the way through and overcoming evil, are made new." (Benedict XVI, *Jesus of Nazareth I* (New York: Doubleday, 2007) pp. 158–159).

The twentieth century, scene of so many advances for humanity, nevertheless brought an unbearable number of acts of injustice—many of them highly cynical, performed in the name of freedom and progress. As the century drew to a close, it became more and more apparent that judicial solutions and economic reparations were not enough. Genuine healing must engage the radical dignity of every human being.

This means concentrating more on the victim than on the perpetrator. When the damage is irreparable or very intimate, the conclusion of the process is far removed from reparation. The extermination camps, the ethnic conflicts in Africa, the war in the Balkans, and terrorism are clear illustrations. In recent years, public opinion, especially in the West, increasingly has seen forgiveness as the most fitting—and at times the only—solution to particular injustices.[18]

In the East, forgiveness forms part of the system of justice. One who breaks the law has departed from the constituted order of society. Since this fracturing of society is seen as something bad, it is fitting that there be a possibility of repentance and,

18. "To ask for and to offer forgiveness is a profoundly noble way for man and, at times the only way, to emerge from situations marked by ancient and violent hatreds" (St. John Paul II, Message for the World Day of Peace, January 1, 1997).

following just punishment and authentic reform, forgiveness for the offender and his reintegration into society.

FORGIVENESS IN THE PRINCIPAL RELIGIONS

The world's principal religions see forgiveness as something good, even necessary, although from different viewpoints and with different limits. All encourage asking forgiveness when one has inflicted an injury, being open to forgiveness when one has suffered an injury, and asking for forgiveness from a deity when we are aware of having transgressed divine norms. Punishment and compensation are recognized as part of the process.

Buddhism considers forgiveness as something necessary to maintain internal equilibrium. It eliminates thoughts that could endanger one's current internal well-being and have a lasting negative effect on one's *karma* [state of soul]. Those damaging thoughts—rancor, hatred, desire for revenge, and so on—are confronted from two perspectives: relinquishing anger and resentment toward anyone who has offended me, and letting go of any kind of compensation for the offenses received. The first perspective interrupts the cycle of injury-pain immediately after the pain in order to prevent it from feeding on itself. The second perspective seeks to prevent vengeance and reinforce gratuitousness.

On the other hand, simply adopting positive thoughts and emotions—such as compassion, compassionate joy, equanimity, friendliness, and loving-kindness—as if nothing had happened does not enrich the relationship. The one doing the forgiving needs to "freeze" the vicious cycle and put an end to it. Although this method can be helpful in achieving peace, well-being, and mental health, it doesn't correspond exactly to true forgiveness.

Forgiveness also exists in the framework of Judaism, although in this case established norms limit the possibilities for granting it and specify its indispensable conditions. Historically, as stated before, the Hebrew people were guided, among other principles, by the Law of Talion (summed up in the expression "an eye for an eye, a tooth for a tooth"): "He who kills a man shall be put to death. He who kills a beast shall make it good, life for life. When a man causes a disfigurement in his neighbor, as he has done it shall be done to him, fracture for fracture, eye for eye, tooth for tooth; as he has disfigured a man, he shall be disfigured. He who kills a beast shall make it good; and he who kills a man shall be put to death" (Leviticus 24:17–21). The point of the law is not to encourage vengeance—as if it were something good—but to promote justice.

Later rabbinic interpretations insisted on the key role of repentance (*teshuvá*) in order to obtain forgiveness. Sacrifices were not enough, nor was reparation for the injury. In the case of offenses to one's neighbor, divine forgiveness was subordinated to that of the person offended. "If the injured party refuses to forgive even when the sinner has come before him three times in the presence of others and asked for forgiveness, then he is in turn deemed to have sinned."[19]

The norms for obtaining *teshuvá* are more demanding when the offense is deliberate. In the era of the Temple, on the Day of Forgiveness or Yom Kippur, a scapegoat was killed to purify the people's sins, but this custom envisioned a collective *teshuvá* or repentance, which is not what is in question here. In the ten days before the Day of Forgiveness, each person was to make acts of personal repentance and ask forgiveness of those whom he or she had offended; positive acts to repair the evil committed were recommended. Without these acts of repentance and asking forgiveness, the Day of Forgiveness would lose its efficacy.[20] And the more understanding an individual

19. Midrash Tanh. Hukkat 19.

20. Curiously, on the day of burial, a representative of the community asks forgiveness publicly from the deceased for the offenses he might have suffered from them.

is toward others, the more understanding Yahweh will be toward that person.

Islam teaches that Allah is "the merciful one" and thus the original source of all forgiveness. This requires forgiving offenses, although, depending on what one has done, the forgiveness can come directly from Allah or from the injured person. According to the Koran, there is only one sin that Allah never forgives: conversion to another God, unless the convert returns to Islam and sincerely begs forgiveness. In principle, the attitude the Koran recommends toward the unfaithful is not violence but, to the extent possible, forgiveness; it defines believers as those who "avoid sins and vice, and forgive when they are offended." The Koran also recognizes that is reasonable to administer a just punishment to the offender and that one who pardons will be compensated by Allah. The problem arises from different interpretations of the Koran, since there is no single source of interpretation. Varying interpretations in turn account for Islam's major limitations on forgiveness, which reach their extreme in Islamic fundamentalism.

The Old Testament contains frequent references to God's forgiveness. There are many instances in which the repentance of man who has acted badly is depicted as capable of changing God's decision. God's infinite justice and mercy are often cited.

Certainly, however, God's forgiveness requires sincere repentance and, in most cases, the giving of penitential satisfaction, usually in the form of sacrifices. But although the goodness and advantages of forgiveness are obvious, references to it and examples are less frequent.

The coming of Jesus Christ brought with it a decisive leap beyond the Old Testament.[21] The Son of God became man and died, manifesting his will to forgive and his infinite love. Forgiveness witnesses to the fact that good—love—is stronger than evil—sin.

Offending another person is also an offense against God, and therefore we must ask forgiveness of both. God instituted the sacrament of reconciliation, whereby, through the absolution imparted by the priest, we obtain divine forgiveness and the security that accompanies it. The phases of the process of forgiveness correspond to those of this sacrament—sorrow for the injury caused, its manifestation, determination not to repeat it, and reparation. If God's love is infinite, all is forgivable. Assuming we repent, God's attitude is one of lasting and unconditional forgiveness.

21. A good summary of the vision of forgiveness in the Catholic Church is found in numbers 2838 to 2845 of Part IV: "Christian Prayer," in the *Catechism of the Catholic Church*.

Forgiveness among men now has a new dimension we could call superabundance, which mirrors the forgiveness of God.[22] Christian forgiveness, far from forgetting or repressing the pain or sorrow, needs to recognize the truth in order to forgive. As St. John Paul II said: "This does not mean forgetting past events; it means re-examining them with a new attitude and learning precisely from the experience of suffering that only love can build up, whereas hatred produces devastation and ruin."[23]

As for revenge, the Christian goes far beyond the so-called logic of returning an injury to the "logic of love," which leads to loving one's enemies.[24] This does not mean renouncing justice, as St. John Paul II points out in the encyclical *Dives in Misericordia*: "It is obvious that such a generous requirement of forgiveness does not cancel out the objective requirements of justice. Properly understood, justice constitutes, so to speak,

---

22. "The discoverer of the role of forgiveness in the realm of human affairs was Jesus of Nazareth. The fact that he made this discovery in a religious context and articulated it in religious language is no reason to take it any less seriously in a strictly secular sense." Hannah Arendt, *The Human Condition* (Chicago: University of Chicago Press, 1958, 2nd. ed., 1998), p. 238.

23. St. John Paul II, Message for the World Day of Peace. January 1, 1997.

24. ". . . I haven't needed to learn how to forgive, because the Lord has taught me how to love." See Josemaría Escrivá, *Furrow* (New York: Scepter, 2002), no. 804.

the goal of forgiveness."[25] Once more we have superabundance—in this case, of justice. Not only must one seek to carry out what is recognized by civil law, but one must also strive for a greater justice: that of forgiving the one who has done evil. For a Christian, this "seventy times seven" forms his attitude of imitating Jesus (see Matthew 18:22).

Another aspect of superabundance is separating the offender from the offense. Here the Christian treats the offender as the child of God that in fact he or she is.[26] One ought to pray for an offender, since one wants God to pardon him. Gratuitousness is also part of superabundance, since, if it is born of love, it does not demand anything in return, inasmuch as God probably has forgiven me more. Empathy and understanding are poor in comparison to loving someone who has offended me. The victim forgives and prays for the offender that his or her heart be converted and, consistent with being a child of God, not repeat the offense.

---

25. Pope St. John Paul II, *Dives in Misericordia*, 14.

26. "In the economy of the gift there is a superabundance which exceeds the ethical; the other is then my equal or my neighbor, the object of solicitude, respect, and admiration; he or she is loved in spite of their shortcomings, one does not expect them to change in any way, and one gives one's forgiveness freely . . ." H.L. Cervantes, *Algunas Consideraciones a Partir de la Antropolgia de Paul Ricoeur* (Leipzig: Academica Espanola, 2011), p. 66.

CHAPTER 2

The Process of Forgiveness

Guilt must be worked through, healed, and thus overcome. Forgiveness exacts a price—first of all from the person who forgives. He must overcome within himself the evil done to him, he must, as it were, burn it interiorly and in so doing renew himself. As a result, he also involves the other, the trespasser, in this process of transformation, of inner purification, and both parties, suffering all the way through and overcoming evil, are made new.

—Benedict XVI, *Jesus of Nazareth*[1]

On the morning of July 30, 2009, the Basque separatist group ETA murdered two young police officers in Palmanova, Mallorca: Diego Salvá and Carlos Sáenz de Tejada. It happened to be the day Diego returned to duty after

1. Benedict XVI, *Jesus of Nazareth I* (New York: Doubleday, 2007), pp. 158–159.

a prolonged absence due to a traffic accident that had left him in a coma for several weeks. Montserrat, his mother, recalled how happy he was to return to work and said that "the sorrow and pain of his absence will not be forgotten nor can it be erased, but one learns to live with it as does a person who is left blind by an accident." She added: "One cannot live with hate. To live with hate is to live in a prison cell, from which one wants to be freed as soon as possible. Prison is for the murderers. I don't want it for myself nor for my loved ones. I decided one day to forgive, and it has done me a great deal of good."[2]

To forgive is first of all a decision, an act of the will, but the reality is more complex and not merely a single act. It is necessary to want to forgive, but on occasion that is not enough. Forced forgiveness—forgiveness by the fast track, so to speak—easily ends in failure. When one is acting merely from a sense of obligation, the result, instead of peace and freedom, can be rage, impotence, and a desire to forget.

Forgiveness can be understood as a response to a particular offense, carried out in phases that are part of a process. But it can also be seen as a habitual

2. In that same interview she said: "On the other hand, I think that it is proper to a mother to give life, to transmit life. It is not right for her to transmit hatred, rancor, and revenge. That only generates sorrow and death. I refuse to transmit this to my family." (See "Interview with the mother of Diego Salve," *http://www.elmundo.es/elmundo /2010/07/25/baleares/1280054911.html.*)

disposition, either within a special relationship with someone else or as a general and universal attitude.

In this chapter, we shall look at the process of forgiveness in stages, more or less lengthy according to the person and the offense. It is possible to get bogged down in a particular phase, in which case pain and resentment are increased by the failure to forgive. At other times, people opt for a substitute for forgiveness, and the result is usually not so positive. These are individuals who justify a hurt or deny it, or they deliberately overlook it because of the perceived difficulty of moving forward. But some people forgive almost at once. These tend to be people with a great capacity for love, such as a mother or a father who forgive each other or forgive their child.

The phases of this process are varied, according to its sources. Some, though useful, are not strictly necessary for the success of the process. In the most common model of forgiveness, someone produces an injury and someone receives it; the process of forgiveness then proceeds in eight steps.

EIGHT STEPS TO FORGIVENESS

1. *Recognizing and identifying the injury.* I am conscious that someone has injured me, although I may not yet know who. I intuit that the injury was inflicted with bad intent. I might renounce vengeance, but I cannot ignore the truth of what has happened or the pain it caused. To forgive requires an effort of introspection in response to the internal convulsion produced by the injury. If the injury is small and causes minimal harm, it probably does not need to be forgiven.

This first step involves "evaluating the damage." Ideally this involves distinguishing emotionally between the injury and the aggressor, which helps in objectifying the injury and calling it by name, while at the same time, making it harder later to identify the offense with the offender. Objectively confronting the injury is very important to forgiving it.

This objectivity is modified by human subjectivity so both the pain and the resentment that follows may depend more on the emotional response of the injured party than on the injury itself.

2. ***Separating the injury or the aggression from the aggressor.*** One evaluates the aggressor in order to determine his or her motives.[3] According to that assessment, it will be easier or more difficult to make progress in the process of forgiveness.

3. "Real forgiveness means looking steadily at the sin, the sin that is left over without any excuse, after all allowances have been made, and seeing it in all its horror, dirt, meanness and malice, and nevertheless being wholly reconciled to the man who has done it." C.S. Lewis, *The Business of Heaven* (San Diego: Harcourt Brace Jovanovich, 1984) p. 62.

3. ***Deciding whether to forgive and renounce revenge.*** I now know the injury and have made a preliminary evaluation of the aggressor. At the same time, I continue to feel the pain intensely, reminding me I have to decide. I can opt for revenge to express hatred, or I can try to forgive. Choosing revenge or resentment is more frequent than it appears. By such a choice, the victim becomes an offender and the offender a victim. One takes on two roles simultaneously: victim and victimizer. There is also an intermediate option: to be injured without wanting either to forgive or receive compensation.

Those who opt for revenge tend to remember the injury received, thus feeding the cycle of pain-injury along with bitterness and a desire for revenge. These negative emotions are a direct consequence of the injury received and the pain experienced. Pain is necessary for forgiveness to have substance, but with the pain come other negative emotions—hatred, humiliation, rage, and so on—which must be eliminated in the course of the process.

There is no possibility of forgiveness if someone forgets the injury and the negative emotions associated with it. What occurs with forgiveness is that, having acknowledged the negative emotions, one chooses to overcome them by renouncing revenge. Desires or impulses toward revenge may not be entirely eliminated and may return, but one who determines that he or she wants to forgive opens the way to overcome them.

4. *Deciding to dignify the aggressor.* After the decision not to take revenge, the real work begins. Drawing on my resources of love, understanding, and benevolence, I must freely reach out to the one who has hurt me. Replacing pain and opposition by surprising the offender with a gesture of *rapprochement* is not easy. On the contrary, empathy, opening the heart to communicate with the aggressor, is one of the most difficult steps in the process and presupposes a prior intention to *dignify the aggressor.*

Some might not want to consider the intentions of the aggressor, but usually this is not so. When I analyze the motivation of the offender, attribution comes into play: to *attribute* is to apply deeds or qualities to someone or something without having certain knowledge. It can be external or situational (based on some external aspect) or internal or dispositional (based on a feature or an intention of the aggressor).

We generally tend to attach more value to internal attributions, which makes forgiveness more difficult. For example, one might think, *He was late for lack of interest* rather than *He must have run into heavy traffic.* One can also generalize about singular events ("He's always late" instead of "He was late this time") and attribute global traits instead of specific ones ("Not only is he habitually late—he lacks class").

This assessment can help me understand that the pain I have suffered arises in part from my feelings, but perhaps the other party has no reason to know how much suffering he or she has caused me. This helps me distinguish the offender from the offense. In a famous open letter to the Nazis, Albert Camus wrote: "And, despite yourselves, I shall still apply to you the name of man. We are obliged to respect in you what you do not respect in others."[4]

Behind the aggressor is a person with the capacity to change and no longer be an offender.

This new relationship framework, enriched by restoring dignity to the offender, indirectly enriches and gives dignity to the one who forgives. Not confusing the guilty with the guilt is the basis of the moral value of forgiveness and fosters a renewal of the heart.

The greater the offense is, the more difficult it will be to restore dignity to the offender. But once I have confronted my own capacity for engaging in a similar act of aggression and set aside both the injury and the desire for vengeance, I have transformed destructive power into a constructive force of rapprochement and potential mutual enrichment.

---

4. Albert Camus, *Letters to a German Friend* as found in *Resistance, Rebellion, and Death: Essays* (New York: Knopf, 1961) p. 30.

5. ***Repentance on the part of the aggressor.*** While not strictly necessary for forgiveness, repentance does help greatly. Above all, it helps if the aggressor sincerely expresses sorrow for the injury inflicted. This must include the clear acknowledgment of his responsibility along with sorrow.

Besides underlining the separation between the aggressor and his or her action, repentance enables the victim to empathize with the aggressor's pain and share the essence of forgiveness—conversion of heart.

Repentance also is limited to the injured party's need to protect himself against the aggressor. It corresponds to the emotional need for at least a gesture—ideally, a promise—offering assurance that the offense will not be repeated.

6. ***Experiencing a change of heart.*** With or without express repentance, at this point there is a transformation in the person who forgives, called *a change or conversion of heart.*[5] Sometimes the moment when one forgives is obvious, but at other times forgiveness takes place in a gradual manner. As one's heart is transformed, the resentment or rejection of the

5. Christian tradition uses the Greek term *metanoia,* which literally signifies "a change of knowledge" but has been applied to the change or conversion of heart in its deepest and most profound meaning. This *metanoia* does not always have to proceed from a feeling of guilt or repentance, but it does have as its end a change for the better.

other person disappears. I undo the knot tying me to the offense I have suffered. This is a real transformation accompanied by positive thoughts about that person—without denying the evil reality of the injury—along with positive feelings that make me find the offender more likable (or at least more possessed of dignity) and actions consistent with this.

7. ***Establishing a new relationship.*** Conversion of heart can be expressed simply in healing wounds and restoring the previous state of affairs, but it can also involve enrichment of the former relationship—or even the establishment of a new relationship. Like forgiveness itself, this usually has an emotional component but also something more. Shaping this new relationship requires at least a minimum of flexibility and creativity. Aggressor, victim, and the relationship between them all undergo an enhancement of dignity.

8. ***An clear manifestation of forgiveness by the one offended.*** To be sure, one can forgive someone who is not present, even someone who has died, but when it is a question of generating a new and richer relational framework, it makes sense for there to be a formal, external expression of forgiveness. Love and forgiveness tend to manifest themselves.

Ideally, it should remain clear that one has suffered pain and injury, but these have been freely forgiven, trusting that the act will not be repeated. This should be done with a humble attitude, without moral superiority; the one who forgives is aware that he or she has benefited from being forgiven on other occasions. I'm saying to my offender that I have forgiven him—I believe he is capable of being absolved, and if he separates himself from his act and recognizes his guilt, he will free himself from the bond tying him to what he has done. At the same time, I have freed myself from that same bond.

CHAPTER 3

Who Can Forgive?

"At last, he mercifully heard my complaints, and wanted to console me with his own: a judge who has been a delinquent, how easily he forgives!"

—Calderón de la Barca[1]

Forgiveness is an act of the will: In the face of an objective injury inflicted intentionally by another person, someone decides freely to repay the offender with a gesture of understanding and love that erases the stain of the injury and can fortify their relationship.

It seems obvious that only persons can forgive. And since a free act is involved, the one forgiving must have a capacity to understand the injury and recognize the offender. The one who has suffered the injury must do the forgiving, not a third party. But can one forgive in the name of another? Can a group of people pardon one or more individuals? And what about forgiving oneself?

1. Calderón de la Barca, *La Vida es Sueño*, Act III.

COLLECTIVE FORGIVENESS

Although forgiveness is essentially personal, the majority of grave offenses are produced collectively. At times, an individual injures a group of people, such as a terrorist who makes an attack that has multiple victims, but forgiveness here can be viewed as the sum of the individual forgiving acts by each one injured.

It is more complicated, however, when a collective entity attacks another: a society forgives a group of evildoers, one country forgives another, etc. In such cases, can there be shared responsibility? How does one judge and forgive? Must the whole group make reparation? Who decides when satisfaction has been made for the injury? Some sociological studies suggest that most people see it as possible for a group of persons to forgive another group of persons. As in the case of personal forgiveness, a declaration—in this case formalized—of repentance and concrete reparation (which does not have to be proportional to the damage inflicted) can be very useful. It is also helpful if the collective entity that is forgiving makes some public declaration—a manifesto or a statement bearing many signatures, for instance.

A fairly recent example of collective forgiveness is a letter Pope Benedict XVI wrote on March 19, 2010, to the Catholics of Ireland and especially the victims of sexual abuse by representatives of the Church in the past. The pope joined in the plea for forgiveness so as to encourage those injured to forgive, proposing that all involved enter into a process of forgiveness involving "cure, renewal, and reparation"—relief of the victims' pain, renewal of the offenders' hearts, along with reparation to confirm and close the process of forgiveness.

The letter's tone was noteworthy. This was a public document written in a deeply human and emotional style.[2] From the first lines ("I am deeply dismayed"), the pope empathized with the victims: "You have suffered grievously and I am truly sorry. I know that nothing can undo the wrong you have endured. . . . No one would listen. . . . You must have felt that there was no escape from your sufferings."[3]

Benedict XVI repeatedly makes reference to feelings and emotions in order to join himself to the victims' sufferings. These affirmations of sorrow in turn foster compassion among those who have to forgive.

Since the crimes were committed by third parties, and Benedict XVI's letter was written as the highest representative of the Church, he could not

2. Another good example along these lines was a homily of Pope St. John Paul II on March 12, 2000 on the Holy Year's Day of Forgiveness.

3. Benedict XVI, *Pastoral Letter to the Catholics of Ireland*, 6.

expressly ask the victims to forgive him. He therefore urged those who committed crimes to pledge repentance, assume responsibility, clearly manifest sorrow, and make reparation insofar as possible for the injury inflicted ("You must answer for it before Almighty God and before properly constituted tribunals").[4] Finally, he proposed certain realistic steps to prevent what had happened from happening again.

Another example is a declaration of Secretary of State Hillary Clinton in October 2010 concerning a 1946–48 study carried out by the Public Health Service that involved inoculating subjects in Guatemala with sexually transmitted diseases. The text recognizes the objective injury ("unethical," "appalling violations," "abhorrent practices"),[5] and expresses her regret. It also offers guarantees that nothing of this sort will ever happen again.

DOES IT MAKE SENSE TO FORGIVE MYSELF?

It is sometimes said that a person needs to learn how to forgive himself. By definition, however, one person can only be forgiven by another—namely, the one whom he or she has injured. To speak of

4. Ibid.

5. *http://www.state.gov/secretary/20092013clinton/rm/2010/10/148464.htm.*

forgiving oneself implies a distorted notion of forgiveness. This makes it worth considering the circumstances in which people generally speak this way.

When I have done or neglected to do something involving injury to myself. For example, perhaps I failed a course because I failed to study. In this case, I can be sorry I did not fulfill my responsibility, and I can repent of the damage I have done myself. But who forgives me? In these cases, the process is not one of forgiveness but of accepting responsibility in a mature way. Repentance culminates in a decision not to repeat what was done.

When, in spite of my efforts, I have not accomplished something I resolved to do and felt I could accomplish. In this case, there is neither responsibility nor guilt, and it is even less proper to speak of forgiveness. One must simply accept one's limitations. There is no place here for forgiveness or even for repentance. True, when dealing with someone who lacks self-esteem, one may indeed encourage him to "forgive" himself. But even so, this is an improper use of the expression.

It seems to me that the concept of forgiving oneself emerges from a psychology of "goodness" that tries to assist people confronting their own guilty behavior or their limitations by pretending nothing is wrong. It is a kind of emotional salve that eliminates the objectivity of forgiveness and pumps up the ego. In short, it is a mistake to speak of *forgiving oneself* rather than *repenting of or taking responsibility for something* or *accepting ourselves as we are.* To accept oneself does not mean to resign oneself, though; in fact, self-acceptance is necessary in order to be able to change.

CAN I FORGIVE IN THE NAME OF SOMEONE ELSE?

On November 14, 2003, Britain's *Daily Telegraph* carried news of a surprising ceremony on the opposite side of the world. In Nubutautau, a village in Fiji, a ceremony took place in expiation for events that took place in 1867.[6] The inhabitants of the village, who were cannibals (which was common in Polynesia at the time) had killed and eaten a Methodist missionary named Thomas Baker and seven native converts. Present at the ceremony of expiation were descendants of the missionary and the prime minister of Fiji. The inhabitants of the

---

6. *The Telegraph,* "Fijians killed and ate a missionary in 1867. Yesterday their descendants apologized," Nick Squires, November 14, 2003. *http://www.telegraph.co.uk/news/worldnews/australiaandthepacific/fiji/1446723/Fijians-killed-and-ate-a-missionary-in-1867.-Yesterday-their-descendants-apologised.html.*

village read a manifesto asking forgiveness from the families of the victims and offering them presents. The repentance of the Fijians was accepted by the missionary's family frankly and without reproach. One of them said the memory of that tragedy had been like an oppressive weight for his family, and the ceremony had provided a new beginning.

While only the one who has suffered an injury is competent to offer and grant forgiveness for that harm, nevertheless if the injury has been inflicted on a person very close to me, I also in some way might be suffering and thus can forgive the offender, whether the person who received the injury has forgiven it or not. For example, when someone injures a child, his or her parent shares the injury and is in a position to forgive the aggressor. Obviously, injury received by a third party is not equal to injury received directly; thus these are two different, though equally valid, ways of forgiving.

CHAPTER 4

The Object of Forgiveness

"Part of every misery is, so to speak, the misery's shadow or reflection: the fact that you don't merely suffer but have to keep on thinking about the fact that you suffer."

—C.S. Lewis, *A Grief Observed*[1]

A few years ago, the Italian press was filled with the story of Pietro Maso.[2] In 1991, when only nineteen years old, Pietro and some friends murdered his parents in order to get their money. He was a spoiled child who spent his money recklessly and wanted more. An expert who evaluated him for the court noted his narcissistic, egocentric personality. Pietro himself said: "That day I entered the tomb together with my mother and father."

1. C.S. Lewis, *A Grief Observed* (San Francisco: HarperOne, 2009).

2. Raffaella Regoli, *Il Male Ero Io* (Milan: Mondadori, 2013).

His two sisters, Nadia and Laura, were shattered and didn't believe they could ever forgive him. But with the aid of a priest who did not give up Pietro for lost, the passage of time, and their religious convictions, they eventually accomplished what had seemed impossible: the conversion of heart of all three siblings. Seventeen years later, his sisters were able to forgive him and rebuild their relationship with the brother they had considered lost.

Forgiveness is directed to an *objective* evil caused *intentionally*, but not to the offender's intentions, which can never be fully known.[3]

The sorrow that leads me to forgive can arise from an objective offense, the pain of which I exaggerate, or from an imaginary offense where in reality there is nothing to forgive.

But in genuine forgiveness, I forgive an objective injury, intentionally inflicted. When I see that an injury came about unintentionally, it is more accurate to speak of *excusing* rather than *forgiving.* One excuses the innocent but forgives the guilty.[4]

It makes no sense to forgive before the offense is committed, even if the aggressor has made it clear he intends to commit it. Until one has felt the pain,

3. The repercussion of the evil act on the offender can only be repaired by the aggressor himself.

4. In traumatic circumstances that unleash a pathological reaction, one of the characteristics of the trauma that makes it more grave and harmful is the perception of malice or bad intention.

one cannot really forgive. Besides, to merit being forgiven, the offense must have at least a minimal reality.[5] The evaluation of offenses differ from person to person, with some giving more importance to disloyalty and others to disrespect.

Are there, however, truly unpardonable deeds, acts that are "radically evil," which make forgiveness impossible? What makes an offense unforgivable? *Unforgivable* suggests a tension between forgiveness and justice that seems oppose forgiving. This "unforgivableness" comes either from the person who has to forgive or the character of the injury—for instance, rape, torture, terrorism, etc. One might suppose that it is the quantity or quality of the offense that makes it unforgivable. But who makes that determination? And are we not here speaking of *irreparable* offenses rather than *unforgivable* ones?

On the other hand, the intensity of the injury and the character of the offender affect each other. If the offense is small, it's easier to forgive a beloved person to whom one is committed than an unknown person, but when the offense is very grave, this order can be reversed. In either case, offenses that involve an attack on one's physical, psychological, social, or moral integrity ordinarily require forgiveness.

---

5. In this sense, Derrida considers that "there is only forgiveness where there has been something unforgivable." Jacques Derrida, *On Cosmopolitanism and Forgiveness.*

One might also suppose that conspicuous voluntariness and intentionality would render an offense *unforgivable,* as the two phenomena—offense and forgiveness—were the same reality. But forgiveness presupposes objective evil, and it is only later that one can forgive. Others consider the absence of express repentance a cause of "unforgivableness." For the victim to forgive the other in such cases seems like self-disrespect.

Another aggravating condition is clear irresponsibility on the part of a committed person—for example, an act of medical malpractice that causes direct physical harm to another. Also to be considered is whether the negative effects of the offense are lasting.

Finally, it is useful to remember that the object of forgiveness presupposes the subjectivity of the offense: If one insults a group of people, some may see themselves as more hurt than others, and the group's various members will forgive the offender more or less according to how injured they feel. Their feelings will in turn be influenced by mitigating or aggravating factors such as their sense of humiliation.[6]

6. Anger is stronger if I feel myself to be held in contempt by the one who injures me. But if someone overcome by pain insults me, it does not anger me so much. Ridicule is more tolerable coming from someone who mistakes me for somebody else; but when I perceive the disdain as aimed directly at me, I flare up immediately.

Nadia and Laura could scarcely see how Pietro could have been capable of murdering his parents for money. Only by coming to understand his immaturity and the attractive power exercised upon him by evil—along with his repentance and their affection, together with the faith of them all—could they reach the point of forgiving him.

CHAPTER 5

What Forgiveness Is Not

"Forgiveness is more a matter of sharing than of granting"
—Jutta Burggraf[1]

In writing about forgiveness, people often explain at length *what forgiveness is not*. Besides being a way of approaching a complex reality, this suggests the frequent misuse of the term. Let us turn to that now.

I will forgive but not forget; I will forget but not forgive. To forgive someone, I must be aware of the injury he has done me and must recognize my own negative reactions: hatred, rage, humiliation, and so on. Moreover, forgiveness requires knowing and remembering the injury, and therefore is the opposite of forgetting. In any case, when one speaks of forgetting, one does not really mean that the deed has disappeared from one's mind; and if that does

1. Jutta Burggraf, "Aprender a Perdonar" in *Retos de future en educación* edited by O.F. Otero (Madrid, 2004), pp. 157–182.

happen—for example, amnesia resulting from an accident—I am then incapable of forgiving the now-forgotten injury.

In some situations the passage of time helps a person overcome his anger or negative emotions without a process of forgiveness. Then it is time, not forgiveness, that heals, and there is no alteration in his attitude toward the injury or its negative value for him. In this case, the expression "I have forgotten, but I have not forgiven" would be perfectly valid, because if I have forgotten, I cannot forgive. Forgiveness is not reducible to the disappearance of emotions, any more than a wound is healed when it stops hurting.

It is important that my relationship with someone who harmed me should not deteriorate after I forgive him, for then it would be as if nothing had happened, and the forgiveness would be a matter of feeling more than will.

The expression "I forgive, but I do not forget" can contain a trap. "I do not forget" can express a decision and be an assertion that I do not wish to break the bond to the injury received.[2] In this case, forgiveness would no longer be a process of healing; it would be the imperfect forgiveness of someone

2. In the words of a famous American preacher of the nineteenth century, Henry Ward Beecher: "'I can forgive, but I cannot forget,' is only another way of saying, 'I will not forgive.'"

excusing an injury—up to a point—without really meaning to wipe away the offender's guilt: a forgiveness without forgiveness.

In summary, forgiveness is an act of the will in which *one wants to forget* but which does not guarantee success in doing that. If that is the case, I must continue calmly in the effort to forgive, counting on time to bring about the ability to forget. The acid test of genuine and complete forgiveness from this perspective is that remembering what happened does not revive the pain, and I am able to treat the offender as I treated him or her before the offense.

Forgiveness and denial. "Defense mechanisms" is the name we give to all those attitudes, feelings, and thoughts that we involuntarily put into operation in response to a psychic threat with the object of providing an adaptive response. These are repetitive strategies, automatically activated, that everyone develops over time. Since they are automatic, there is no guarantee they will work; indeed, a defense mechanism can involve attitudes and behaviors that are ineffective or even pathological.

Teresa is happily married and the mother of four children. She came to consultation seeking help with tensions building up in her daily life. At the beginning of her marriage, her work as a secretary was readily compatible with her duties at home.

With the arrival of children, however, she found she couldn't take care of everything and became more and more tense and tired. Recently she'd had various fainting spells that her family doctor, after tests, attributed to stress.

At the first consultation, it was obvious that, along with an actual increase in her work and family tasks, she was naturally disposed to experience tension.

She was very demanding of herself: she needed to make sure everything was in order before she was able to fall sleep, kept turning worries over in her head, and was a perfectionist. As her husband said, "She cleaned what was already clean." As the consultations continued, it became increasingly clear that insecurity and low self-esteem caused her to make demands on herself to compensate for deep guilt feelings. These feelings had persisted since she was a child and had become deeply rooted. Although she said she did not recall anything of her youth, gradually, as if not wanting to accuse anyone, she remembered that, despite ill health, her mother raised eight children, of whom Teresa was the oldest. Her father, a businessman, spent much of his time, including weekends, away from home. Her mother suffered dizzy spells and often had to stay in bed; years later, she learned that her mother had migraine headaches.

Teresa educated herself and demanded much of herself. She became a "second mother"—essentially she had no adolescence. When her father came home, he would ask her: "How is your mother? Is everything in order?" Now she saw clearly how that had influenced her. She felt both proud of being her parents' support and angry about all those joyless years. It was beneficial for her to speak of those things she "had almost forgotten" in a mood of security and confidence, and she was able to forgive her parents, both now deceased. She finally understood that they contributed to her self-reproach and perfectionism but were not "guilty" of having caused it.

Where forgiveness is concerned, the most significant defense mechanisms are negation, repression, and projection. *Negation* means the person semiconsciously denies reality—in this case, an offense. This is not the same as excusing something or lying about it.[3] Something similar happens with repression, which involves sweeping something "under the rug." In both cases, someone dismisses from consciousness images, feelings, and memories that are

3. The classic definition of falsehood is saying or doing the opposite of what one understands to be the truth or what one says one will do, with the intention of misleading. As a defense mechanism, the intention is not exactly to deceive, although that might happen, but to relieve oneself of a burden.

painful, sorrowful, or unacceptable, forgetting—or almost forgetting—them.

The defense mechanism of *projection* involves attributing the cause or the guilt for something to another person or circumstance so one doesn't have to confront one's own responsibility.[4] In these cases, one makes an effort to set aside the offense, because one is suffering a pain one cannot bear or does not want to bear, instead of undertaking a process of forgiveness. Such an individual puts on blinders so the sorrow doesn't "distract" him. In failing to confront the reality of the injury, one deprives oneself of the possibility of forgiving.

Not consciously aware of the injury suffered, I do not see the need to forgive, and it remains like a foreign body within me, rendering me unable to forgive. While I may be counting on this foreign body remaining permanently sealed off, the reality is that, although I neither see nor hear it, it still *hurts* and affects my relationship with everyone linked to it.

Unlike repression, negation, and projection, *simulation* is not a defense mechanism. Here the person consciously pretends there has been no injury and

4. Other more pathological mechanisms proper to situations of psychotic depersonalization, such as long captivity or torture, are the identification with the aggressor or acceptance of the mistreatment as something deserved.

no pain and mimics forgiveness. But it makes no sense to justify or excuse the other person so as to ignore the pain. At best, one who does this loses the opportunity to forgive and delays the healing.

These three interior defense mechanisms are different ways of fleeing reality and denying pain. But pain denied always reenters as if through a back door. Confronting suffering in an adequate way is indispensable to achieving interior peace.

Forgiving is not a renunciation of our rights. When I forgive a person for a specific act, I do it freely. I make good use of one of the possibilities offered by freedom: the right to forgive another person. One who is not free cannot forgive.

Forgiveness goes beyond what is demanded by strict justice. It does not annul justice but exceeds it. It is different not merely in quantity but in quality. I have a right to be respected, but if someone fails to respect me, I have the right to forgive him. This is in no sense the situation of someone who forgives only because he thinks himself unable to vindicate his rights, for such a person would not be exercising freedom but rather extending a false forgiveness.

On the other hand, I can forgive a person who has injured me while at the same time demanding that he or she satisfy justice and carry out the appropriate sentence, if any. If I do not take justice into consideration, I fail to weigh the objective burden of the injury, which makes it difficult or impossible to pardon the person while prolonging the pain precisely because justice has been left undone.

Forgiving is not a demonstration of moral superiority. The thumbs-up of a Roman emperor is an act of clemency rather than true forgiveness. It might be an expression of magnanimity, but it might also express arrogance. It is perhaps best described as an indulgence, in the dictionary's sense of "the inclination of persons to forbear, tolerate errors, or grant favors."

To pardon a punishment is not the same as forgiving. And telling an offender, "You may wish to offend me, but you lack the ability to do that," may be a way of returning an insult, but it is not forgiveness. In the same way, calling the offender ignorant may perhaps lessen one's pain, but the other person is humiliated rather than forgiven. As Oscar Wilde shrewdly remarked, "Always forgive your enemies. Nothing annoys them so much." One who forgives exhibits a high level of morality and an interior strength that should not be confused with a display of power or superiority over another. As Jutta Burggraf puts it, "I forgive you the offense you have given me as the offender that I also am. Forgiveness is more to share than to grant."[5]

Forgiving is not simply a decision, not a pure act of the will. The decision to forgive can go against the current of one's emotion—sorrow or anger—but it is not a matter of making up one's mind to forgive and doing so in response to a legal or categorical imperative. Forgiveness should be voluntary but not *voluntaristic.* It involves intelligence, memory, imagination, and sensibility. Someone must *want* to do it inasmuch as it requires going beyond mere justice. For the process to work, there must be a kind of "starter" that overcomes inertia and resists the negative dynamic of aggression.

It is the person as a whole who forgives, purifying memory, controlling imagination, and making an effort more fully to know the personal reality of the offender. When I say, "I forgive you," this helps me to forgive, but the words are not enough. Appropriate behavior is also required. A child is able to give and receive forgiveness just by kissing or being kissed by its mother.[6] This sort of *magical forgiveness,* purely voluntaristic in an adult, is far from genuine forgiveness.

---

5. Jutta Burggraf, "Learning to Forgive," Almudi document, 2004.

6. It is like saying "Be healed, be healed" over a bruise, with surprising emotional results even though the swelling continues.

Forgiving is not a kind of amnesty or condoning. Although one can use the term *forgive* in reference to amnesty, it is really the *suspension of a punishment for an external motive.* The expression "grant amnesty" indicates its character as an impersonal exercise of authority. It is not a process of forgiveness among persons involving guilt and repentance.

One way of condoning is to see an objectively damaging action as a mere *lapse,* a *technical error.* Forgiving then is implicit recognition that no evil occurred, and there was nothing to forgive.[7] As Jankelevitch points out, this is not forgiveness; it is making an "intellectual excuse."

In general, *to grant amnesty* or *lift a punishment* does not constitute an act of forgiveness in the true sense, and in fact could impede forgiveness or be a poor imitation of it.

To forgive is not to remain imperturbable. Nirvana or pure stoicism, supposing it to be a real possibility, would rule out both suffering and forgiveness. Not feeling physical or emotional pain might even prevent the detecting of injury.

The act of forgiving does not mean everything becomes as it was before. Forgetting, as we have seen, is a

---

7. Vladimir Jankelevitch, *Forgiveness* (Chicago: University of Chicago Press, 2005).

characteristic of authentic, consummated forgiveness. It involves living with and relating to the other party "as if nothing had happened." But this does not always take place. The scar caused by the offense may still trouble me, despite my best efforts to make it otherwise. I would only be making things worse by telling myself I no longer harbored negative feelings. Doing that would distance me from the freedom I need to move forward by forgiving. Moreover, after forgiveness, things are *not* just as they were before. I am a better person, the dignity of the parties is enhanced, and my relationship with the one who offended me may actually be stronger than ever.

Forgiving is not the same as reconciling. Reconciliation is an act between protagonists of a relationship that has weakened or broken who decide to restore it. In many cases, it requires forgiveness of one or both, according to their view of what has occurred. But one can forgive a person without wishing to restore the previous relationship. There also are cases, especially those involving physical or sexual abuse, in which there is no interest in reconciling as long as the offender does not change his attitude. It also is possible to preserve a relationship with an offense not yet forgiven and to forgive someone with whom one is no longer related, as happens in forgiving an offender who is now deceased.

Finally, forgiving is more than just a moral obligation. Only if I see forgiving as a manifestation of love can I be said to have an obligation to forgive. But in that case it is a moral obligation and, like love, must be satisfied freely. Otherwise it is neither love nor forgiveness. Forgiveness is not genuine if not free. I may strongly desire to forgive someone I love, but I have not yet managed to do it. Similarly, I can attempt to treat someone who has injured me as I did before but achieve that only superficially or not at all. In this case I must be satisfied with treating him with the respect he deserves.

CHAPTER 6

Characteristics and Attitudes of the One Who Forgives

"He who is devoid of the capacity to forgive, is devoid of the capacity to love. . . . Forgiveness is a catalyst creating the atmosphere necessary for a fresh start and a new beginning."

—Martin Luther King Jr.[1]

Forgiveness can be considered as something that takes place at a particular moment or as a process over time. One can also distinguish between forgiveness as an act and an attitude. Some people have a habitual tendency to forgive, encouraged by their values and beliefs, although they do not always manage forgiveness.[2] This attitude is part

1. Martin Luther King Jr., *Strength to Love* (Minneapolis: Fortress Press, 2010), pp. 44–45.

2. Some authors propose the term "spiritual intelligence" to cover a capacity to forgive based on understanding, gratitude, and humility.

of their capacity to forgive. Efforts have been made to measure that capacity, involving the evaluation of its cognitive, emotional, and behavioral aspects. But one's capacity to love remains the most decisive factor at the moment of forgiveness. Along with it, one's capacity for understanding, self-knowledge, and generosity also predispose one to forgive.

CHARACTERISTICS OF THE PERSON WHO FORGIVES

That everyone can forgive and be forgiven does not mean that forgiving makes the same demands on everyone or that everyone succeeds equally well at it. In fact, there are some people for whom it apparently comes more easily. But why? Were these people born that way? And if not, can the ability to forgive be acquired? What personality features or abilities increase the capacity to forgive?

Many studies agree that women have a greater capacity and a better attitude toward forgiveness. The authors suggest this may be due to the greater capacity for empathy women possess and their tendency toward acceptance due to their maternal instinct. Men, on the contrary, tend to use more mechanisms of negation or rationalization in the face of the same situations. Some studies have found that the capacity to forgive increases over time, possibly in relation to moral and cognitive development. Finally other studies suggest that religious faith and the presence of children are associated with forgiveness.

Although some authors regard the predisposition to forgive as innate and inherited, I consider it to have moral and emotional origins arising from the desire to be on good terms with others and, in the case of believers, with God. This predisposition is not enough. One learns to forgive by forgiving, and one's maturity is proportional to one's ability to forgive. A person with a weak ego suffers more from being injured, tends to take refuge in fantasy, and has less capacity to forgive. The capacity to love is crucial, so that the capacity for love and the capacity for forgiveness appear as two sides of the same coin.

Let us turn now to some relevant personality traits.

Highly sensitive people suffer more from offenses and are more likely to feel resentment. This greater sensitivity has a positive aspect: It may prompt forgiveness in order to recover emotional stability.

On the other hand, those who are highly sensitive may become more focused on the pain of an offense—and on the offender—which makes the process of forgiveness more difficult.

A special variety of sensitivity is interpersonal sensitivity, the tendency to interpret all experiences in light of interpersonal relationships. "Why didn't she look at me?" or "Why didn't they call?" or "Why don't they notice me anymore?" Such distrust or paranoia causes a person to feel aggrieved, to perceive negative intentions in others' behavior, and so on. The ability to forgive is reduced, and the tendency to experience resentment increases.

Neurotic and/or narcissistic people tend to perceive injuries as more severe and find it harder to forgive. Other people manage their emotions well, see them for what they are, express them and resolve them adequately. They therefore generate fewer negative emotions and tend to forgive more readily.

Highly sensitive people have abrupt emotional swings. They can become extremely angry or offended for a short time, but eventually they return to their previous emotional state and turn the page. Biology and acquired character traits both play a role in this.

People with a more secure style of attachment enjoy a greater disposition for forgiveness. They are more open to what they share in common with other persons, put the person above the pain, feel compassion for the aggressor, and take a more positive view of renouncing revenge and restoring relationships. Their sense of security reflects their early closeness with their parents, especially their mother.

The capacity for empathy also has importance, since it enables us to put ourselves in the place of the offender, understand his emotions, and get at least a sense of his motivations. This assists the process of attributing dignity to him and achieving mutual compassion.

When a person tends to interpret others' behavior positively, he or she is more predisposed to forgive.

People with more imagination do more fantasizing. This makes it harder for them to set aside feelings and confront the objective situation, a necessary step in facing the injury and the pain, and so being able to forgive.

Egocentrism likewise makes it difficult to look objectively at the offense and the offender with the intention of empathizing, having compassion, and forgiving. The egocentric individual is more likely to cling to his sense of victimization.

Low self-esteem and emotional dependence, frequently found together, contribute to the fragility of the ego and create obstacles to gratuitous forgiving.

The tendency to dwell on what has happened tightens the knot of the injury-pain loop and keeps emotions alive and inflamed. This tendency to ruminate is related to insecurity, which makes it difficult to make decisions and take actions—in this case, the process of forgiveness.

Also important is the injured party's capacity to analyze the situation, evaluate the injury, and weigh the pros and cons before making a decision to act. It makes a big difference if the person was educated in a setting, especially a family, where he or she experienced forgiveness, saw its benefits, learned how to forgive from his or her parents, and practiced it in everyday life.

The change of heart that forgiveness supposes requires sufficient flexibility to admit the possibility of change. Along with flexibility, a certain creativity is needed in order to reformulate one's relationship with the person who inflicted the injury.

PERSONALITY TYPES

Our personality is composed of a variety of features present in various degrees. These features determine modes of perception and confrontation of vital circumstances, along with the way we see ourselves and relate to others. The task of forgiving is more or less difficult depending on one's personality type.

The narcissistic personality involves a notable incapacity to forgive. People with this personality trait overvalue themselves and expect or demand special treatment. Along with their air of superiority, they are often envious and lack empathy and the ability to put themselves in another's place. They tend to exploit others without offering anything in exchange and have a volatile self-esteem that accounts for their hypersensitivity to rejection or offenses. When criticized they react with rage and sometimes aggressiveness, they show a low tolerance for disappointment and mistakes, and they exaggerate their capacities while minimizing their defects.

Vengeful gratification and revenge are the narcissist's most frequent response to offenses or injuries. When they have acted badly or made a mistake, they adopt rationalizing strategies (i.e., justifications) that allow them to bounce back or blame others. They tend to exaggerate offenses because the offenses are against themselves. The intensity and duration of their resentment is therefore greater, and their superior attitude makes true forgiveness difficult. At most, forgiveness is granted as an exercise of power and is more like an act of clemency. Narcissism is the virtual antithesis of the capacity to forgive.

The paranoid personality is very sensitive to slights and setbacks. Someone with this personality is rancorous and finds it difficult to forgive. Suspicious, this type of person tends to interpret external stimuli badly and is often jealous. The practice of attributing evil intent to people's behavior frequently causes the paranoid individual to feel resentment. By storing up negative judgments and interpretations, such a person creates a system of suspicion through which everything that comes his or her way must pass. Slow to forgive lest they appear weak and manipulable, such people react to the harm they anticipate at the hands of others, not out of narcissistic self-absorption but in response to the "bad intentions of those who want to harm me."

Obsessive or bipolar personalities also have trouble forgiving. Highly sensitive, they tend to suffer more pain from offenses. They are usually rigid and have difficulty changing, are legalistic and moralistic, and suffer more from injustices. This leads them to demand numerous guarantees that those who hurt them truly repent. Their obsessive character makes it difficult to undo the knot of damage-pain-revenge. Nevertheless, their moralistic tendency impels them to do just that. In the same way, they can demand more by way of reparation and can experience tension between their sense of duty to forgive and the difficulty they experience in doing so.

MORAL ATTITUDES THAT LEAD TO FORGIVENESS

According to authors like Jutta Burggraf, four moral attitudes have major implications for the capacity to forgive.

1. Love

Forgiveness is an act of love. In many cases, success in forgiving depends on loving intensely. As the poet Werner Bergengruen puts it, "Love is proved by fidelity and is completed by forgiveness."[3] When one forgives someone he or she loves, forgiveness flows more easily, almost spontaneously. But when the offense is grave or the person who caused the injury is not yet a loved one, it is necessary to call upon one's capacity to love.

In Teresa's case, her affection for her parents was decisive. Her interior conflict resisted the closing of the wound, but the parents whom she loved and the childhood years during which she felt responsible for her mother's health and the smooth functioning

3. Cited by Burggraf, "Aprender a Perdonar."

of the household had conditioned her to feel that she mustn't fail. With her conscience relieved of those pressures, she felt a certain frustration and anger about her "lost" childhood. But whose fault was that?

Forgiveness can be considered the highest manifestation of love, a gratuitous gift of something one does not have to give. It can transform the hearts of the one who forgives and the one forgiven. But if someone has offended me deeply, I may not be able to love at once and may need to separate myself emotionally from the aggressor for a time. This emotional separation may also involve physical separation as a prerequisite of wholehearted forgiveness and eventual love.

As for the one who has committed the offense—or feels himself guilty—it's important to remember that to live and develop in a healthy way, one must be accepted just as one is. This means someone must love that person and tell him or her, "It's good that you exist" despite limitations, mistakes, and misdeeds. We are all offenders. Love expressed through forgiveness makes us conscious of our value and our beauty, things basic to our self-esteem and the development of satisfactory relationships. If I am not forgiven, I am deprived of the space in which to live and develop; unable to fulfill myself, I am spiritually killed or mutilated.

2. Understanding

Harmony between an offended person and an offender calls for understanding. Realizing that we all need more love than we deserve, I want to forgive you despite what you have done.

Living through her own stress helped Teresa understand her mother's limitations and bad health as well as the worries of her father, who frequently had to be away from home in order to maintain his family and was obliged to depend on his oldest daughter. This understanding strengthened her will to forgive.

Forgiving presupposes a firm conviction that behind the evil someone has done is a vulnerable human being like oneself and, also like oneself, capable of changing—a person worthy of being forgiven, somone whom I can forgive. An obtuse individual, excessively demanding of others or prone to take himself too seriously, may refuse to forgive. But if you want someone to be good, treat him as if he already were.

3. Generosity

To forgive requires a generous and merciful heart that goes beyond justice. The space where forgiveness exists is precisely where punishment does not cover the loss. This does not mean canceling one's right but transcending it.[4] Forgiveness is by nature unconditional, gratuitous, and unmerited. In forgiving someone, I wish that person well. Here gratitude enters the picture as a social by-product of forgiveness. When A does something good for B, B should return the favor as a matter of justice. But if B, besides repaying the debt, then does A a favor out of gratitude, A may then be grateful in return and look for ways to respond in kind. Thus a social network consisting of debts of gratitude is created that generates a permanent benevolent attitude among the persons involved. In this manner forgiveness creates a climate of forgiveness. One who has been forgiven is more disposed to forgive, and one who has forgiven sees more clearly that he needs forgiveness from others.

There is, however, a wrong way of forgiving. This is strategic or pedagogical forgiveness: "I forgive you so that you reflect on what I have done and mend your ways." Such forgiveness is not bad, but it does not measure up to forgiveness in its fullest sense: forgiving you because, in at least some aspect, I love you despite the real

4. "Be convinced that justice alone is never enough to solve the great problems of mankind. When justice alone is done, don't be surprised if people are hurt. The dignity of man, who is a son of God, requires much more." St. Josemaría Escriva, *Friends of God* (New York: Scepter, 2002), no. 172.

harm you have done to me. What is more, I can forgive another without the person knowing it, as a gift. Even though being forgiven or observing someone who forgives from the heart can be the greatest lesson of a person's life, the pedagogical effect upon the offender is not of the essence of forgiveness.

4. Humility

Prudence and sensitivity are needed to express forgiveness. There is no certainty what the response will be, and someone who forgives makes himself vulnerable to more pain. Thus, if time has passed since the offense occurred, it is important that there be a space for me to explain what moved me to forgive and listen to what the other party has to say—and also to what he or she does not say—and thus get as close as possible to his perspective.

To forgive is an act of interior strength, but not of power. I should forgive as the offender-sinner I am, not as though I were sinless myself. The trajectory of forgiveness tends outward and is freeing, whereas that of damage-pain-revenge tends to retreat inside and is constraining. We all do damage, and therefore we all need to be forgiven.

Can My Capacity for Forgiveness Be Measured?

In the last two decades, some standards have been proposed by which someone's capacity for forgiveness can be measured, with varying degrees of success.

Some of these measuring tools are designed for use in the face of a specific event, such as the Transgression-Related Interpersonal Motivations Inventory. This scale assesses the tendencies to seek revenge and avoid the offender, as well as the attitude of benevolence. Others focus more on the relationship of couples: the Interpersonal Resolution Scale. The Transgression Narrative Test of Forgivingness measures capacity using five fictitious scenarios. The Enright Forgiveness Inventory, perhaps the best known, evaluates cognitive, emotional, and behavioral aspects of the capacity to forgive.

CHAPTER 7

The Other Side of Forgiveness: The One Forgiven

"How guilt refined the methods of self-torture, threading the beads of detail into an eternal loop, a rosary to be fingered for a lifetime."

—Ian McEwan, *Atonement*[1]

Forgiveness is possible only in an environment of freedom, and therefore it is a personal reality, centered on the one who has suffered the injury. But that does not prevent the aggrieved or offended party from having an important and sometimes decisive role relating to repentance and seeking forgiveness.

We have seen the part repentance played in Nadia and Laura's forgiveness of their brother, Pietro, for the murder of their parents. The women

1. Ian McEwan, *Atonement* (New York: Anchor, 2003), p. 162.

could not understand how their own brother, so protected by their parents, could have been capable of this atrocity. For years the most they could do was avoid him and not visit him in prison. With the help of a priest, however, Pietro experienced conversion and deeply repented of what he had done. Now he began to show his repentance and beg their forgiveness sincerely and persistently, until, with the passage of years and helped by their faith, they decided to forgive him. Pietro's sincere repentance made his sisters' forgiveness possible, or at least made it easier.

REPENTANCE

The dictionary's definition of the act of repentance—"being sorry for having done something"—seems rather thin in view of the richness and complexity of content the term covers.[2] To see this, one need only read Max Scheler's monograph on repentance, which I used in writing this section.[3]

Many modern authors consider guilt and repentance to be negative phenomena. They hold that someone who feels he has done something bad need

2. In Latin, *doleo, poenitet, piget,* or *taedet* (which refer to being hurt, being weighed down, or something that is painful or tedious) all signify repentance.

3. Max Scheler, "Repentance and Rebirth" found in *On the Eternal in Man* (New Brunswick, NJ: Transaction, 2010).

only do a better job next time. They even argue for a certain determinism in the conduct of people who avoid responsibility and therefore guilt for what happened.[4] They consider repentance to be as absurd as tearing a page off a calendar or turning back the hands of a clock—an attempt to wipe out the traces of a crime.

But, they point out, there is no way of wiping out the act itself, which has passed. Other authors, such as Nietzsche, consider repentance an interior deception arising from hatred or revenge for a bad conscience—a subtle or perfectionistic form of self-punishment.

So what is repentance? It can be defined as *a pronouncement of the moral conscience that leads to self-healing when I recognize my fault for having done some injury—to another person or myself—and am led to have compassion for the person injured and to desire not to do it again.*

According to Max Scheler, failure to understand repentance usually comes from a poor understanding of how the mind works. Those who say it is absurd to try to annul something in the past think of life simply as a sequence of events occurring one after another. This is the case with inanimate nature, but human beings can make moments from the past

4. Viktor Frankl says in *The Unheard Cry for Meaning*, this pan-determinism serves as an alibi for criminals (New York: Simon & Schuster, 1978, p. 50).

present again at any point in their lives. Past, present, and future are all contained in some way in each moment to the extent it partakes of the value of one's whole life.

But any reliving of the past also remains incomplete in value and meaning until one's death. One can always give a new value and meaning to one's past deeds. As Scheler puts it, "Historical reality is incomplete and, so to speak, redeemable."[5] I can repent of something in the past and give it new meaning, freeing myself from the pain of guilt—and recognizing my present history can free me from the hold that the history I lived in the past has upon me.

To those who believe that repenting of something in the past makes no sense, it is enough to say we do not change the act, which remains in our memory, but we do change its meaning and value.

Other authors, following Spinoza, consider repentance something wretched and impotent, and reduce it to mere *fear*. But fear is always directed toward a danger that has not yet arrived, and while it is true that fear sometimes causes repentance, more often it contaminates it. Fear is a premonition of a future menace, but repentance is necessarily retrospective.[6]

---

5. Max Scheler, op. cit, p. 41.

6. François de la Rochefoucauld refers to this fear when he says: "Our repentance is not so much regret for the ill we have done as fear of the ill that may happen to us in consequence." *Maxims*, no. 180.

Therefore Max Scheler says, "Repentance is not a psychic burden, nor a self-deception; nor is it a mere symptom of a lack of psychic harmony nor an absurd shock of our psyche against what is past and unmodifiable."[7]

Also essential to the understanding of repentance is guilt. In a society like ours, where feelings play an exaggerated role, many people identify guilt with a mere feeling. But guilt is a moral quality originating from one's own bad deeds. Someone who says, "I am not conscious of any fault, therefore I have nothing to repent of" is merely betraying his ignorance of the essence of guilt. If a crime has been committed, its perpetrator is guilty whether he feels culpable or not.

Sensitivity in perceiving guilt varies from person to person and also in oneself over time. As Scheler puts it, "Part of the darkest efficacy of guilt is that as it grows it hides itself and dulls one's feelings," whereas a person's goodness refines sensitivity to the feeling of guilt.

Repentance is not directed at the feeling of guilt but at an objective quality truly present, even though the guilty act may have taken place in the past. It does not erase the act and its real consequences, but it can erase the guilt, thus breaking the

7. Max Scheler, op. cit., p. 116.

bond by which guilt had kept one chained to the past. As forgiveness breaks the cycle of pain-injury from the side of the victim, so repentance breaks it from the side of the offender. Repentance looks to the past with sorrow, but it takes a joyful stance toward the future. As Scheler says, "The most revolutionary force of the moral world is not utopia, but repentance."

Repentance is more than just one's guilty conscience and sense of remorse. It has three stages: first, the recognition of the negative character of a morally bad act; second, pain or sorrow for the act; and third, the desire or intention not to repeat it.[8] A guilty conscience is the recognition of the bad action, with or without sorrow and frequently tinged with anger or annoyance, which makes it difficult to be sure of its source. In remorse, the discomfort is greater, since the person has not succeeded in repenting and broken free of the bad action. Instead, he or she experiences additional feelings, data, judgments, and so on, as if in a flood that drags with it all kind of objects and sometimes a corpse or two.[9] In both cases, recognition of guilt and perception of

8. This is another way of viewing positive psychology's four phases of positive acceptance: intellectual acceptance of what has been lost; emotional acceptance, with sorrow; adjustment; and moving ahead.

9. Repentance can be made more difficult by suspicion that the victim is exaggerating the injury—playing the victim—and perhaps provoked it.

the damage caused are both obscured. The result is a mix of emotions that make it difficult to displace the guilt from the vital nucleus of the experience. In both cases—remorse and bad conscience—the flurry of emotions scarcely allows room for compassion toward the injured party and a freely willed determination not to do it again.

ASKING FORGIVENESS

As we have seen, it is helpful, though not essential, that the offender ask to be forgiven. It is good that the evil be recognized and, to the extent possible, repaired.

For the one offended, the request for forgiveness is important in making the decision to forgive. In the opening stages of the process of forgiveness, the offended individual must restrain the instinctive response in the direction of revenge and instead seek to consider the dignity of the aggressor, separating the reality of the person—who is good, after all—from his or her objectively bad acts. The request for forgiveness presupposes that the aggressor feel compassion for the victim, so that the sorrow is now shared by both.

But sometimes there is no request for forgiveness. The aggressor is not repentant or has died or is unknown. Then it is naturally more difficult to forgive.

From the point of view of the one who committed the injury, asking for forgiveness is a logical consequence of his repentance. What matters most in the healing of guilt is repentance, not least because often there is no opportunity to seek forgiveness. In formulating his request, the offender puts a distance between himself and his unjust action, while at the same time assuming responsibility. A genuine request for forgiveness makes it clear that the offender has put what he did (and his past as well) behind him.

If the request is authentic and translates into clear repentance, offender and offended plainly have something in common: both reject the negative moral value of the offense and the evil it inflicted. Here is where an incident narrated by Simon Wiesenthal becomes relevant.[10] He was called upon by a dying German officer who, conscious of his guilt for past deeds which caused him daily suffering like a kind of martyrdom, felt compelled to ask forgiveness of a Jew. Wiesenthal was rather cool, but apparently the German officer was consoled by having made the request. Another illustration occurs in Peter Weir's film *The Way Back*.[11] The protagonist,

---

10. Simon Wiesenthal, *The Sunflower: On the Possibilities and Limits of Forgiveness* (New York: Schocken, 1998).

11. *The Way Back*, Peter Weir, 2010.

deported to Siberia unjustly on the basis of his wife's testimony obtained by torture, makes his escape and travels on foot across the whole Asian continent. In a moment of exhaustion and crisis, he recognizes that he is duty-bound to make this effort in order to give his wife, whom he still loves, an opportunity to ask his forgiveness and be forgiven, thus freeing herself from an emotional bond forcing her to undergo a Calvary like his.

WHAT IS THE PROCESS OF ASKING FORGIVENESS LIKE?

One might think the positions of aggressor and victim are absolutely opposed, and the characteristics and dispositions for forgiving therefore are completely different from those of asking forgiveness, That, however, is not the case, at least not entirely so. I speak elsewhere of the moral attitudes that facilitate forgiveness: love, generosity, humility, and understanding. While generosity is not part of asking for forgiveness, the other three are.

Ordinarily, someone who is strongly conscious of having been forgiven will be more understanding and more moved to forgive. He may be expected to be well aware of human weakness—both his own and others'—as well as of the dignity of the person, the greatness of love, and the freedom that allows him to escape the perverse dynamic of the injury-pain-revenge cycle.

It can also be equally or even more difficult to ask forgiveness than to forgive. For example, the aggressor may feel that the victim is exaggerating what happened to him, perhaps overreacting to obtain some advantage, or he may think the other provoked him, since otherwise he would never have done what he did. This naturally makes repentance more difficult or dilutes it to the point of being ineffective.

The process of asking forgiveness involves the following steps:

1. Recognizing that one has caused an injury or given offense. Initially internal, this recognition tends to manifest itself.
2. Making an effort consistent with one's emotional resources to understand and feel the other person's injury and pain and mention it in the request for forgiveness.
3. Recognizing the role played by circumstances in the aggression and the reaction to it, without ignoring the fundamental reality: the injury that has been caused. Leaving aside any extenuating circumstances, I now want to ask forgiveness. This is not a judgment but a request.
4. Requesting forgiveness should express repentance clearly. This expression, however it is done,

should leave the receiver with no doubt concerning what is being expressed.

5. It can be helpful to assure the injured party that his reluctance to forgive is understandable. The point is to make it clear that one does not consider oneself merely to have made a mistake or a technical failure: "I know I injured you, and I am sorry. I ask your forgiveness."
6. Make restitution or repair the damage to the extent possible. It is good to ask, "Can I do anything for you?"
7. Suggest devising a plan or some steps one can take so the act will not be repeated.
8. Allow the person who has extended forgiveness henceforth to occupy the place in the relationship that he or she prefers. This can be done while at the same time making it clear that one would like as far as possible to restore the relationship to its previous state.

CHAPTER 8

Imperfect Forgiveness Is Still Forgiveness

"But ever since that moment I have realized afresh that no guilt is forgotten so long as the conscience still knows of it."

—Stefan Zweig, *Beware of Pity*[1]

FROM GRATUITOUS FORGIVENESS TO THE QUID PRO QUO

One of the essential characteristics of genuine forgiveness is its gratuitousness. "You did me an injury, and although pain and anger instinctively lead me to seek revenge or at best cut myself off from you to avoid possible future injury, I have decided to forgive you. I am doing this because I want to. If I succeed, it is better for me—and possibly for you (if you repent). I forgive you as an exercise of freedom, not out of a sense of obligation. Your repentance

1. Stefan Zweig, *Beware of Pity* (New York: New York Book Review Classics, 2006), p. 353.

would be helpful to me since it would imply an intention not to repeat what you did, and that would make it easier for me to open my heart. But I repeat that I forgive you because I want to, and it is not necessary that you accept my forgiveness or promise not to do it again."

But those who see repentance as necessary to forgiveness argue that the one who caused the injury was the one who broke or damaged the relationship, and so should be the one to take the initiative in reestablishing it. The majority of those who have written on this subject agree for one reason or another on the necessity of repentance. But even so one must insist on the gratuitousness of forgiving lest we have here simply an exchange of forgiveness for repentance.

Consider the case of Soledad and Sergio described earlier. When Soledad learned of her husband Sergio's infidelity, she seemed to understand that he had repented and was asking forgiveness because he did not want to lose her. He tried to convince her that he had always felt guilty for what he had done and now was even more deeply repentant at seeing her suffering upon learning of it.

Clearly, whatever the offense, the personal qualities of the injured party, and the behavior of the offender, genuine, gratuitous forgiveness can be very difficult—indeed almost impossible to achieve.

But since forgiveness is a process and one can always forgive in the future something one does not now feel capable of forgiving, wanting to forgive is almost more important than actually forgiving. Often the offended party needs something in exchange, a quid pro quo: ideally, the request for forgiveness, a fruit of the offender's repentance, a declaration that the act will not be repeated, or even some kind of compensation or reparation.[2]

FREE AND NECESSARY FORGIVENESS

In principle, authentic forgiveness is extended in perfect freedom. No one is obliged to forgive. The movie *The Descendants*[3] contains a scene in which an outraged wife who has just learned of her husband's infidelity vents her feelings at the woman with whom he betrayed her who is in a coma and dying. Tearfully she says, "I forgive you, I have to forgive you, because I hate you for having tried to take my husband, but I cannot hate you." She realizes that she wants revenge. But what revenge is possible upon someone at the point of death? She has

2. Quid pro quo, to give something in exchange for something else, is closer to genuine forgiveness than *do ut des*—"I give so that you give"—which seems more utilitarian or consequentialist: "I give you my repentance so that you will forgive me" or "I forgive you so that you won't do it any more" or "so that I will feel better."

3. *The Descendants,* Alexander Payne, Fox Searchlight Pictures, 2011.

to forgive the other while there is still time, wanting to free herself from her pain and restore her life and interior peace.

Although at times forgiveness can seem necessary, to accomplish its healing it must be done freely—although this might be nothing more than "I need it, but I'm going to do it because I want to." While the need reduces the authenticity of the act to some extent, enriching the person who forgives less and conferring less dignity upon the person who is forgiven, at times this is as much as someone can manage. This helps us see that, although forgiveness is closely linked to emotions, it is not a matter of feeling only but an act of the will that cannot be reduced to a psychic or emotional state.

In forgiving, an injured person not only forgoes revenge but, as it were, diverts the blow and transforms a negative action toward oneself into something positive for the offender. The energy that accomplishes this transformation comes from within the one who forgives. In some cases it involves a kind of "giving birth," including pain.

CONVERSION OF HEART AND RESENTMENT

Forgiveness works a change of heart in one who forgives. It produces a change in the thoughts, affections, and negative emotions caused by the injury, leading to a new relationship and a new closeness to the one responsible. Someone who forgives remembers the past injustice so that it not be repeated, but he or she remembers it as forgiven.

Negative emotions do not always completely disappear at the end of a process of forgiveness. These emotions are of two kinds: those that accompany the suffering caused by the injury and those perhaps disproportionate but understandable feelings of hatred and desire for vengeance directed at the perpetrator. Feelings of the first sort are progressively transformed, but those of the second are contrary to forgiveness and should disappear. Also, despite having made a clear decision to forgive, one may find that such feelings have not been completely eradicated, and one requires more time and effort to do that. This is when one must accept the fact of one's emotions, follow the rhythm of one's nature, and have patience.

It would be a mistake to consider this situation of having to wait as a failure. Although forgiveness has an important element of feeling, it cannot be reduced to feelings, much less to simple and unmixed ones. St. John of the Cross said that sometimes a wound is so deep that if we can't love the person who inflicted it, it is enough not to wish him anything bad.

Among these emotions and negative feelings is one that we have called understandable but possibly disproportionate: resentment.[4]

Max Scheler calls resentment "self-poisoning of the soul."[5] Left untended, it will persist, weakening the person's ability to resist it. It is toxic to the intelligence, clouding judgment and objectivity, and to the will, making it rigid and incapable of forgiveness. Consciousness of what happened in the past colors everything having to do with the relationship with that person and everything surrounding the offense. Each resentful revisiting of what occurred renews the pain in one's soul and makes it harder to free oneself from it.[6]

As with other negative emotions and feelings, the role of forgiveness is to minimize resentment,

---

4. A dictionary defines *resentment* as "having feelings of grief or anger about something." Other sources define it as "feeling again." In classic Latin it is *exacerbatio animi*: producing bitterness and irritation; see *Nuevo Diccionario Latino-Español Etimologico*, Raimundo de Miguel (Madrid: Visor Libros, 2nd ed., 2003). It is normal to reject and dislike the evil connected with a blow one has suffered, as one would also do if someone else were injured. But when it is oneself, one's natural self-esteem increases the reaction: "I didn't deserve that."

5. Max Scheler, *Das Ressentiment im Aufbau der Moralen* (Frankfurt: Klostermann, 1978), p. 4.

6. "The aggression remains imprisoned in the depth of the conscience, almost unnoticed; there within, it incubates and ferments its bitterness; it infiltrates into our whole being; and ends up being the director of our conduct and of our least reactions. This sentiment, that has not been eliminated, but rather has been retained and incorporated into our soul, is resentment." Gregorio Marañón, *Tiberius: A Study in Resentment* (London: Hollis and Carter, 1956).

beginning with the decision to overcome it. Resentment will be reduced by the intellectual effort to understand the fault through considering the circumstances and by willing one's withdrawal from the cycle of injury-pain-vengeance. Success is not guaranteed, however, least of all in the short run; forgiveness cannot be equated with the disappearance of resentment because, among other reasons, one can never be sure of having entirely succeeded.

THE SUPERABUNDANCE AND ASYMMETRY OF FORGIVENESS

In earlier times, the best one could do upon suffering an injury was to have recourse to justice: "an eye for an eye." And justice is no small thing. Forgiveness only appeared on the scene with the arrival of Christianity. The life and teaching of Jesus introduced something new: *forgiveness in a radical sense.* One of its essential characteristics is its asymmetry, arising from the new and broadened framework established by the one who forgives with the one forgiven.[7] Not only was the memory of what had

7. There is an asymmetry between the one who forgives and the one forgiven, the one who gives and the one who receives. When the forgiveness is adjusted to "the circularity of the gift, the model no longer permits distinguishing between forgiveness and retribution, which makes the two members totally equal." Paul Ricoeur, *Memory, History and Forgetting* (Chicago: University of Chicago Press, 2004).

happened purified, but also this new relationship came into being by the benevolent act of returning good for evil. Forgiveness does not bypass justice or take it lightly; it takes it into account and surpasses it, producing an effect that has something almost divine about it: superabundance.

We say we have something *to spare* when we have more than we need. But superabundance goes a step further; it is the equivalent of having a great deal to the point of profusion. I practice superabundance, as it were—that is, I act in a disproportionate way—when besides making a positive return for something negative inflicted on me, it is clear that I am doing something more than routinely human. The result, too, is surprising: to confer dignity upon both offender and offended and make possible a better relationship.

In this sense, the *modus operandi* of forgiveness resembles that of gratitude. It also involves exceeding oneself. Gratitude disposes me to do more than what is just for someone who does me a favor, and that "more" generates an indefinite sequence of reciprocal acts. In this way one reaches into a future where people give more than they receive and build a better society. Here is the opposite of the injury-pain-hatred cycle, which immobilizes individuals, embitters relationships, predisposes people to revenge, and distorts the perception of past, present, and future.

CHAPTER 9

Forgiveness and Health

"How important forgiveness is, it translates into emotional, spiritual and emotional health, loving is forgiving and forgiving is loving. Love and forgive."

—Carlos Casanti

The close relationship between the mind and body is taken for granted today. Some studies suggest that holding onto negative emotions resulting from offenses received can predispose one to alterations in one's bodily and mental functioning and result in the development of various disorders.

At first sight, it seems reasonable to suppose that persisting in a high level of rage, anger, or resentment will end up harming a person, though the negative effects may be contingent upon a particular individual's psychosomatic constitution. Negative emotions are destructive by reason of their strength and pervasiveness. They allow one no peace. Thus someone so afflicted for a long time becomes more likely to suffer various mental pathologies.

Some develop reactive symptoms, adaptation disorders, become depressed or anxious, or possibly fall into addiction. If prolonged excessively or very intensely, or if the personality is more fragile, these symptoms can become chronic, most usually taking the form of depression. A very special symptom is post-traumatic stress disorder, which tends to become chronic, even though it might be a reaction to a single traumatic event. Its seriousness depends, among other things, on the degree of cruelty and humiliation perceived in the aggression, the sense of helplessness of the one injured, and the intensity of the trauma, together with the personal characteristics of the one who has suffered it. People with a greater capacity to forgive and to ask forgiveness have less pain and resentment, which helps shield them against mental disorders.[1]

Other mental disorders are not entirely the result of an injurious event but reflect a person's biological predisposition, which unleashes a potentially chronic symptom in response to a stressful situation. This sometimes is the case in a bipolar disorder.

---

1. The study of forgiveness has lately been encouraged by the appearance of positive psychology, a branch of psychology that seeks to understand the processes underlying positive human qualities and emotions by using scientific research. It aims to achieve new knowledge about the human psyche, not only for the sake of solving mental health problems but also to attain a better quality of life and well-being (see *www.positivepsychology.com*).

When this happens, the process of forgiveness loses its efficacy once the sickness takes hold.

As for physical health, both anger and anguish release large quantities of potentially toxic hormones into the blood. These include cortisol, adrenalin, noradrenalin, prolactin, and testosterone. All are related to alterations in the physical condition of the organism: changes in cardiac and respiratory function, sleep disturbances, lessening of defenses, and a lower pain threshold. Some studies have found a higher incidence of heart disease in people with a large store of anger and resentment. Others have discerned a correlation between difficulty in forgiving, feelings of rage and impotence, and chronic pain. This last correlation can be due to a greater sensitivity to pain—a lower threshold—or to a failure to confront an issue due to frustration. Still other studies have linked the capacity to forgive to a lesser need for medication.

GUILT, FORGIVENESS, AND PSYCHOTHERAPY

Freedom is exercised in choosing. Realizing I have chosen the better thing, I am happy; I learn from the experience and probably will repeat it in the future. When I have chosen poorly, I repent of my error and try not to repeat it. But often this process is more complex: I realize that in choosing I was moved by weakness to choose what was best for me but worse for others. As Ovid says in his *Metamorphoses,* "I see and approve the better course, but I follow the worse."[2] Now I experience guilt, and the experience has an impact on my feelings of sorrow and repentance.

Thoughts and feelings of pathological guilt accompany mental ills like depression or certain obsessive conditions.[3] These feelings, far from directing behavior, tend to limit it to a greater or lesser degree, and in cases of delirium can remove action from the sphere of conscience.

Some authors liken guilt, which helps one detect poor choices and bad conduct, to physical pain, which alerts one to the fact that all is not well in one's body.[4] Guilt and pain are pathological to the extent that they are effects that exceed their causes. Sometimes pain and guilt exist without any cause—they are false signals—or are disproportionate. But the opposite extreme, some sort of anesthetizing of

---

2. Ovid, *Metamorphoses,* VII, 21.

3. An analysis of conscience and feelings of guilt by Javier Cabanyes, "La Culpa: Mito, Enfermedad, o Realidad," can be found in *Palabra,* June 2013.

4. For this section I have borrowed some ideas from Professor Raphael Bonelli, a Viennese psychiatrist associated with Professor Johannes B. Torello, a disciple of Victor Frankl: "Psicologia de la Confession," in *Palabra,* July 2012.

the body or the conscience, would be an unacceptable alternative.[5]

In view of this provocatively simple account of guilt, why do some schools of thought view it in a negative light? In order to abolish something natural and simple, they deny either freedom, good and evil, or the role of conscience.

For Sigmund Freud to have attacked guilt as a breakdown of the psychic apparatus and something pathological that shuts us off from repentance and rectification made sense from the perspective of his determinism. If freedom does not exist and I cannot choose, I cannot be responsible for or guilty of anything; in that case, guilt is a construct—either pathological and requiring elimination by therapy or an expression of self-interest. The trouble with this view, however, is that, in attempting to free man from the onerous burden of guilt, it makes him a slave of determinism and a victim of others—society, one's parents, one's school, or whatever. Our

5. As the German psychologist Albert Görres, cited by then Cardinal Ratzinger, has said, "the capacity to feel guilt forms an essential part of the heritage of man's soul. . . . The feeling of guilt, which breaks the false tranquility of conscience, is a signal which is as necessary for man as is corporal pain, which allows one to recognize the alteration of normal vital functions. . . . One who is unable to feel guilt is spiritually sick, he is a living cadaver, a mask of character. . . . Beasts and monsters, among others, do not have any feeling of guilt." Joseph Ratzinger, "*Si Quieres la Paz Respeta la Conciencia de Cada Hombre,*" in *Verdad, Valores y Poder* (Madrid: Rialp, 2012).

modern therapeutic culture, in its eagerness to eliminate all pain, functions as a kind of pain killer that fails to heal the wound while compelling one to act as if nothing had happened.

Moreover, if every cause of evil came to me from without, it would seem to follow that I was faultless. Any injury I might do to others would be attributable to some external cause. But this would be to live in a permanent state of self-deception. Strange to say, those who decry repentance as self-deception end up deceiving themselves about their alleged moral perfection, denying or repressing whatever does not fit that story line. At the same time renouncing freedom in favor of determinism makes one a victim of powers beyond his or her control, something difficult to square with one's supposed perfection.

In not a few instances, the underlying reality in cases like this is a sense of inferiority, impotence, or hopelessness regarding any improvement; self-knowledge, self-acceptance, and the possibility of change are blocked. In this sense, as Professor Torello says, humility, based on reality, is the cure for feelings of inferiority.[6] Joy comes to replace hopelessness.

Perfectionism tinged with neurotic tendencies is no help to improvement. Rather, seeing that

6. Johannes B. Torello, *Sicologia y Vida Espiritual* (Madrid: Rialp, 2008).

things are beyond one's control and the exercise of freedom, a person feels more insecure. Soothed by being told that we are not free, that conscience is an invention of Puritans, that there is no good or evil and we are all alike, one comes face-to-face with everyday life and the doubts reappear. Remove the consciousness of true guilt, and a false guilt appears. Ideas like these move people to rebel against their proper purpose in life, converting them into fugitives who seek excuses in their suffering and justification in their pessimism.

This worldview, typically neurotic though somewhat diluted, is widespread in our society. Only in abandoning this attempt to make guilt a sort of pathology does one come to terms with the fact that we all do bad things, and guilt is a moral quality that springs from recognition by conscience of the evil we have done.[7] This frank, direct, and simple recognition of the evil committed resolves the "problem" of guilt without having to renounce freedom, conscience, and the moral value of behavior. I am a good person who sometimes does bad things. When I do, I understand that those acts are the product of my freedom. I accept my responsibility and my

7. In the Catholic doctrine of forgiveness, the importance of repentance is clear from the fact that perfect sorrow, by itself, brings about guilt's remission. (See the *Catechism of the Catholic Church,* 1451–1454.)

guilt, and through repentance free myself. And then I begin again.[8]

Fortunately, more recent therapies, based on a realistic anthropology, seek not to eliminate guilt but to accept it fully.[9] These therapies attempt to take advantage of the feeling of guilt so that the person assumes his or her responsibility, makes correct use of his or her freedom, and takes into account his or her limitations and circumstances.

One can understand, therefore, that pathological guilt, when susceptible to treatment or therapy, is not resolved by denying normal guilt. We cannot reduce normal guilt to the psychological sphere, as is done by some who aim to eliminate culpability. If all guilt were pathological or purely psychological, improvement would be difficult indeed. But when we detect the motives behind this pathologization of guilt—conscious styles of confrontation, unconscious defense mechanisms, and so on—and accept normal guilt for what we freely did wrong, we grow as persons. Persons are free to do good and evil, to make mistakes, to rectify, to ask forgiveness, to forgive, and begin again as often as necessary.

---

8. In one of his *Humoradas,* the poet Ramon de Campoamor writes: "I will paint for you in a song the wheel of life: to sin, to do penance, and then to begin again."

9. This is the case, for example, of Acceptance and Commitment Therapy. See *Terapia de Aceptacion y Compromiso (ACT)*, by Kelly G. Wilson and M. Carmen Luciano (Madrid: Piramide, 2011).

SOME THERAPIES BASED ON FORGIVENESS

Throughout this book we have seen how the capacity to forgive differs among people. The differences are due in part to biological aspects of temperament—such as reactivity to a stimulus—but above all to personality features, personal attitudes, and values. In this connection, special importance must be given to one's early experiences of forgiveness, above all during childhood, as well as to the values one has assumed, or has tried to assume, in reference to morality and living with others. Negative experiences of forgiveness similarly raise obstacles: For instance, when someone who is supposedly repentant asks my forgiveness and then injures me in the same way again.

Most of the capacity to forgive is acquired. In some traumatic situations, forgiveness is an essential part of the process of change and healing, especially in wounded relationships with others. In this regard various protocols have been established that differ in specific details but fundamentally coincide.[10]

Before starting any of these therapies, it is important to conduct a prior evaluation of the

10. A review of the interventions of forgiveness is found in Brad W. Lundahl, et al., "Process-Based Forgiveness Interventions: A Meta-Analytic Review," *Research on Social Work Practice,* 2008; 18:465–78.

"forgivability" of the situation, including the characteristics of victim and perpetrator, their relationship, and of the nature of the offense. With this data the therapist can decide whether it is opportune to seek forgiveness or better not to try. Later the steps of the process should be explained, so that the person will consent freely before undertaking it.

There are various therapy techniques, and here we shall look briefly at two. The first is cognitive-behavioral, and the second is humanistic-existential.

COGNITIVE-BEHAVIORAL TECHNIQUE

This technique was developed by Robert Enright and Richard Fitzgibbons and includes four phases.[11]

The discovery phase consists of examining the offense and detecting the responses to it in thoughts, emotions, and behavior.

At the start, it is necessary with the help of the therapist to detect and recognize the psychological mechanisms of defense adopted in response to the injury. These mechanisms, developed over time, function automatically, with little consciousness that they are operative. It is especially necessary to explore denial, repression, and projection so that the

11. Included in *Helping Clients Forgive: An Empirical Guide for Resolving Anger and Restoring Hope* (Washington: APA, 2000).

person confronts both the offense and his thoughts and emotions. It is particularly important to recognize anger and the sense of injustice by which the individual safeguards his or her self-respect, thereby reinforcing the ego and separating oneself emotionally from the injury so he or she can forgive it.

In some cases—for example, sexual abuse—it is especially important to evaluate the victim's humiliation or culpability. Later it is important to the perceptions of the painful event and its circumstances, along with cognitive distortions such as personalization or "catastrophism" that can differ in the offended person and the offender and have a negative impact on both the present and the future.[12]

The decision phase concerns the "change of heart" discussed earlier. The person becomes aware of his or her negative emotional situation and wishes to change the strategy of confrontation. This decision may be very difficult, given the pain already being experienced and the sense of being treated unjustly. Ordinarily a considerable effort is required to quit the cycle of injury-pain-vengeance.

---

12. Cognitive distortions are systematic errors in processing information. They are produced by the rigid and inappropriate application of preexisting intellectual schemas that bring with them non-adaptive responses. They form an essential part of cognitive therapies, one of whose most important exponents is Aaron T. Beck (*http://www.beckinstitute.org*).

Third is *the work phase*. Here one must make active use of the means to produce real change. First comes "recontextualizing" the aggressor and the aggression, which leads to restoring dignity to the aggressor. Later there is an attempt to empathize with him or her. At this point it is easier to accept the pain of the offense than to attempt, as revenge would suggest, to cause the aggressor pain or redirect it toward someone else. The final step, which cannot always be attained, is to have pity on the offender and even offer him love.

Fourth is *the going deeper phase*. Having advanced in the process, one can discern a greater meaning in the unjust aggression. Forgiving and being forgiven, one sees, creates space for living together. One consults one's feelings at this stage to verify the freedom and enrichment obtained through forgiveness.

This process, presented in twenty steps by the authors mentioned, occurs at different speeds depending on the nature and intensity of the offense and the victim's capacity to change.

THE HUMANISTIC-EXISTENTIAL TECHNIQUE

The humanistic-existential technique has its origin in Viktor Frankl. For this author, the search for meaning is a person's primary motivation. With this psychotherapeutic technique, the therapist helps someone give meaning to his or her existence. One fundamental source of the ability to forgive, to escape the injury-pain-vengeance cycle, is the fact that life has meaning. Frankl maintains in *Man's Search for Meaning*,[13] one of the last century's most influential books, that everyone has his own equivalent of a concentration camp, and to survive it must, among other things, learn patience and forgiveness. Fundamental to doing this is finding meaning in one's life. Forgiving someone who has offended me does not mean being satisfied with being offended; and, indeed, if I am sure of the meaning of my life, I am not satisfied. But it allows me to accept the reality of an injury, to situate it in relation to that meaning, and, if necessary, generate a new relationship within that framework with the person who offended me.

Finally, based on one's knowledge and freedom, and on repentance, guilt can be confronted in a healthier and more positive way within this context of meaning.

13. Viktor Frankl, *Man's Search for Meaning* (New York: Pocket Books, 1959, 1984).

CHAPTER 10

Keys to Forgiveness in Marriage

"There appeared in her eyes a tear
and on my lips a phrase of forgiveness . . .
pride spoke and she dried her tears
and the phrase died on my lips.
I walk along one path, she another;
but in thinking of our mutual love,
I still say: Why did I keep quiet that day?
And she will say: Why did I not weep?
It's a question of words, and, nevertheless,
neither you nor I will ever,
after what has passed, agree
who is the guilty one.
It's a shame that love lacks a dictionary
where one can find out
when pride is simply pride
and when it is dignity!
—Gustavo A. Bécquer, *Rhyme* 30[1]

---

1. Gustavo A. Bécquer, *Rhymes*.

If forgiveness is essential for us as social beings, its importance is greatest in marriage and family life. Some authors even propose a model of forgiveness specifically for couples, especially applicable to situations of severe transgression. Within the richness of the relationship between couples, I want to call attention to two aspects that influence many everyday situations and might provide occasions for forgiveness: the perfectionism of either party and the role of so-called rules of living together.

PERFECTIONISM

Partners in a marriage do not complement each other because they are perfect and have a perfect relationship. Part of what unites them in substance and intention is precisely the mutual help they offer each other for growth. But what if they are perfectionists? By definition, such people make excessively high demands of all aspects of life. As part of a couple, they usually expect the other party and the relationship itself, in its emotional dimensions, to have no defects. But of course that is impossible. If a couple's life together involved no difficulties or conflicts, it would mean they were avoiding problems and fleeing mishaps instead of learning from those experiences. Multiplying conflicts is not a good idea; but no one is free from imperfections, either in oneself or in one's relationships.

A perfectionist also may maintain a defensive attitude in a relationship. This is a result of insecurity and a fear of suffering. Many perfectionists have a high degree of emotional sensitivity, along with insecurity and low self-esteem. Where a defensive attitude is present, it will be more difficult to cultivate intimacy and trust. Finally, if partly due to a defensive attitude as well as the habitual rigidity associated with this personality type, someone refuses to accept the suggestions or corrections of the other party, he or she would lose the opportunity to grow in self-knowledge and improve the relationship. To the extent both spouses confront their conflicts and overcome them, the "immune system" of their relationship is reinforced. The objective is not attaining a perfect relationship, and much less to maintain perfection day in and day out—an unbearable task—but to promote the relationship's maturation and growth as each spouse improves. As this progress occurs, forgiveness is essential to break the cycle of injury-pain as often as necessary and enable the relationship to move forward—from the destructive dynamic of rigidity and impossible perfection to a constructive dynamism.

Not surprisingly, it is hard for a perfectionist to ask forgiveness. Sensitivity and rigidity cause such a person to feel offended more often and more deeply. That makes it more difficult for him or her to forgive. The perfectionist functions more by feelings of duty and, in spite of sensitivity, can occasionally be surprisingly impersonal in making judgments. This makes it harder to have empathy and compassion for someone who asks forgiveness after failing to do what he ought to have done. It may then happen that the perfectionist will require more assurances from the other party that the offense will not be repeated and perhaps also expect the offender to make amends in some way.

VIOLATION OF THE RULES

Men and women normally come to the marriage with certain expectations and desires regarding how they desire the relationship to be—how they want to be treated, what to expect and not expect, and so on. It is important that they come to marriage having clearly expressed those desires and expectations, and as new ones emerge, express those, too. Otherwise there is a danger of these expectations becoming "rules for living together."[2] Sometimes, at the beginning of a marriage, each partner is more ready to satisfy the other's expectations because the

2. Aaron T. Beck, *Love Is Never Enough* (New York: Harper, 1989).

relationship is marked by a more intense experience of love. But as time passes, or with the arrival of children, the romantic love carried over from courtship tends to dissipate, ideas of fairness and duty take hold, and the rules of living together learned in the families they grew up in come into play. People tend to reenact the family patterns they learned as children, including that of their parents' relationship.

Sometimes one partner becomes disproportionately upset at the other's behavior—behavior not particularly wrong in itself but for some reason painful to one spouse. In such cases, a failure to observe one of the rules of living together is most likely involved. This usually is the case in troubled marriages.

Examples of such rules are: "If you really loved me, you would do what I want without my needing to ask you"; "If it really mattered to you, you would know enough to stop working on your hobby/quit watching television/stop talking on the phone when you see I'm overwhelmed"; "If you really cared for me, you wouldn't always allow me to be the one who has to do the disagreeable stuff."

These rules come from the unstated expectations of one spouse. Not expressing them is often accompanied by the failure to take into account the desires and expectations of the other spouse, not giving him or her an opportunity to approve, modify, or negotiate. When one spouse makes a rule explicit, it frequently appears arbitrary or even unreasonable to the other spouse. Besides, these are rules with the character of absolutes: They must always be observed; although they began as desires, they have become little less than unalienable rights, when they are not outright requirements.

Often they are preceded by "If . . .", which sets up a dichotomy: if this is done, good; if not, bad. Tensions grow, as the other spouse has no idea how to handle outbursts provoked by seemingly innocent behavior.

These rules also raise problems of boundaries and limits, especially if the other spouse doesn't know a rule is involved. So, for example, in the face of "If it really mattered to you, you would stop doing X when you see I'm overwhelmed," it's necessary to determine what sort of X is involved, since weekend skiing is not the same as watching sports on TV, nor is going to the pool every other afternoon the same as having coffee with friends now and then.

Even worse, rules over which one spouse has silently brooded can lead to considering certain unpardonable faults. Each time the behavior is repeated, the emotional charge can again cloud the mind of the brooding party, making the violation of the rule more and more intolerable, even though his or her spouse may remain ignorant that there is such a rule.

Although these rules can make a relationship difficult and harden a troubled situation, simply speaking up can undo that knot in the relationship. If that isn't done, frequent requests for forgiveness, even though heartfelt, will progressively lose their authenticity. It is important to share the rules of living together, so that forgiveness can be applied to the objective and subjective injury, with the compassion and empathy needed for authentic forgiveness able to emerge.

Other rules appear reasonable, but making them absolute or punishing a spouse for breaking them gives rise to a cult of duty that distances the couple from their original self-giving and makes their relationship rigid and unstable. I take satisfaction from having my spouse do as I wish, but I should also find satisfaction in doing as my spouse wishes and so making my spouse happy. A wife wedded to a rule-driven way of living together may consider an attack on one of the rules as an attack on herself: "If it really mattered to him, he would give up X once in a while"—meaning: "If he goes out to practice his favorite sport tomorrow (never mind when he last did that), it's a sign that I count for nothing with him." But suppose her spouse leaves work tomorrow burdened with so much job-related irritation and frustration that he needs some recreation so as not to bring it all home and dump it on his wife?

Two people who really love each other can find that situations like this affect them as much as real offenses. But as the old song says, "You only hurt the one you love." In marriage, the relationship is so close that one tends to assign very personal meaning to everyday actions. Thus one can be less tolerant with a spouse than with others. Spouses tend to consider what their spouses do for them as an obligation, ignoring the more profound and essential reality that their spouses are "there" for them freely, even though just now they may be feeling disappointed about something.

In forgiving the violation of rules of living together, it is important that the person offended be explicit about the rule that underlies the feeling of being offended. This will help the one who needs to ask forgiveness understand what he or she did that caused pain, while the one who feels injured can in this way learn the transgressor's intentions. Thus the two will now be in a position to share the sorrow, though each one with his or her particular nuances, and share one another's pain. The process of forgiveness will move ahead, and, to the extent one of the spouses has openly communicated to the other what expectations he or she has regarding their relationship, a satisfactory compromise may now be within reach to smooth the way in the future.